Reclaiming the Future

Reclaiming the Future

A Beginner's Guide to
Planning the Economy

Simon Hannah

Foreword by John McDonnell MP

PLUTO PRESS

First published 2024 by Pluto Press
New Wing, Somerset House, Strand, London WC2R 1LA
and Pluto Press, Inc.
1930 Village Center Circle, 3-834, Las Vegas, NV 89134

www.plutobooks.com

British Library Cataloguing in Publication Data
A catalogue record for this book is available from the British Library

ISBN   978 0 7453 5020 2   Paperback
ISBN   978 0 7453 5022 6   PDF
ISBN   978 0 7453 5021 9   EPUB

This book is printed on paper suitable for recycling and made from fully
managed and sustained forest sources. Logging, pulping and manufacturing processes are expected to conform to the environmental standards of
the country of origin.

Typeset by Stanford DTP Services, Northampton, England

Simultaneously printed in the United Kingdom and United States of
America

You have to act as if it were possible to radically transform the world.
And you have to do it all the time.

—Angela Davis

Well there's a better world that's a-coming ...

—Woody Guthrie

[O]nly a return to utopian thinking can clarify the minimal conditions for the preservation of human solidarity in the face of convergent planetary crises.

—Mike Davis

Everything you see in our town, greenhouses, livestock, all shared.
Collective ownership ... This is a commune. We're communists.

—Maria, *The Last of Us*

I can't let things be this way. We can be wonderful. We can be magnificent. We can turn this shit around.

—Tank Girl

Contents

Acknowledgements

It takes a village to raise a child and this is no less the case for a book. I am eternally grateful to everyone who read over the manuscript or parts of it and gave me feedback; Michael Löwy, Michael Roberts, Alfredo Saad-Filho, Susan Pashkoff and Phil Ward. Graham Balmer for very early comments. Mercedes Ekanem for listening to me read it out. Steven Ellis and Ruth Cashman for my usual thanks with every book. K.D. Tait and Rowan Fortune for their thorough editing of the manuscript. Samuel Robinson for assistance with human nature. Stephen McSweeney for helping me grasp the essentials. Lots of others who helped with various parts. If I have forgotten anyone I apologise unreservedly. Any factual errors are my own, any political errors are up for debate.

Foreword

John McDonnell MP

The regular crises of our economic system have understandably focused the minds of working-class people and their political organisations, on the basics of economic survival, on how to get by, on how to protect and possibly even hopefully improve their living standards.

Political debate remains dominated by questions about the distribution of rewards and wealth. This has long acted as a smokescreen behind which is hidden the more significant debate about the distribution of power. Put simply, we talk too much about wealth and too little about power.

Historically, one can see why. The brutal hardships inflicted upon the emerging working class in the early stages of the industrial revolution prompted the rise of mass trade union movements. The experience of their members of often savage poverty alongside immense wealth exposed the grotesque inequalities produced by the economic system they eventually named capitalism.

It's understandable that the economistic demands for a fairer allocation of the rewards of wealth creation dominated the attention of working-class people and their organisations. It was made obvious by the daily experience of their working lives that workers were not receiving the full benefits of the wealth they produced.

In response, in the fields and in the small workshops of the industrial revolution the workers discovered a secret. It was the secret of solidarity. The secret was written on the banners and in the songs of the trade union movement and is still today.

'Unity is strength.'

'An injury to one is an injury to all.'

'Strength in the Union.'

By using the strength of organised solidarity, the working class found that it had a power that could influence by negotiation the distribution of the rewards of capitalist production. It fell to the early socialists to transform both the political discourse and strategy of working-class movements with an analysis of the origins and exercise of power under capitalism.

The history of the socialist movement has been, from then on, a debate about how power can be gained and how it can be organised and exercised in the interests of the working class. At the core of this discourse has been the concept of planning.

The advocates of capitalism extol the setting free of uncontrolled animal instincts, combining to create the hidden hand of the market as the optimum method of economic decision making. Whilst socialists, recognising the chaos and crises this leads to, have looked to reason and rationality to control and plan economic processes. The reality is that planning has been an inherent feature of capitalism but it has been used to plan for profit maximisation and not to satisfy need.

This well-timed book charts the seeds of this debate and goes on eloquently to describe the different approaches to planning that historically have been promoted and undertaken.

The value of this work is twofold. First, the widespread recognition over the last four decades that our world is on the edge of climate catastrophe has added a completely new and urgent relevance to the argument for controlling and planning our economic activities.

Second, if socialists and progressives are to succeed in developing and securing the means to plan our economy to tackle the climate emergency and to overcome the divisive, destabilising inequalities of our society, they need to be armed not only with an understanding of the arguments for planning but also with a knowledge of the history of experience of planning methods, both successes and failures.

To organise and mobilise the social movements we need to face up to and overcome these critical challenges we need cadres that have a deeper understanding of the methodology of change. This book greatly assists in putting that knowledge and understanding in the hands of those would be cadres of transformative change.

Introduction

Our society is sick. It is unsustainable, volatile and violent, producing a devastating ecological crisis. We have built a world where corporations and businesses dominate and exploit us to enrich the wealthy and powerful who control the economy. Capitalists exploit planet and people. We are set to work extracting from the planet so they can extract profit from us; we do not control our existences beyond the occasional vote for parties that primarily maintain the status quo. Governments drive down corporation tax while shareholders hoard trillions of dollars in offshore bank accounts, then governments plead poverty makes them unable to tackle any social issues.[1] Capitalism built cities, roads, railways, and aircraft, towering skyscrapers alongside luxury yachts, but leaves many of us clinging to life. We are in an era of social disintegration.

The climate crisis is already here. The planet is dangerously heating due to our economic activity. Alongside the usual pollution associated with mass consumer production, greenhouse gases released through energy production accelerate ecological breakdown. Mega-fires are devastating swathes of land, there is regular flooding of major cities and water reserves are depleted. We have already overshot the 1.5°C target, while politicians luxuriate with hoping to phase out fossil fuels by 2050. The average polar ice caps shrink yearly, allowing petrochemical companies to prospect for new oil and gas reserves.[2] Melting glacial ice is shipped to cocktail bars in UAE for the rich.[3] Eighty-one per cent of fish stocks have been depleted since 1970. Every human on the planet has Teflon in them.

Many of us have microplastics inside us. The profit motive causes a murderous rift between people and planet but pollutes us both. In response companies gaslight and manipulate us, hiding the truth behind greenwashing. Petrochemical companies have covered up knowledge of anthropogenic global warming since the 1970s.[4] For many, the high water is here. For others, hell is around the corner. Future generations will live on a ravaged and devastated planet, but no doubt say, 'At least we made money for the shareholders.'

Today, capitalism has outlived its usefulness. It pumps out commodities that quickly end up in landfill. New technology has built-in obsolescence to ensure endless consumption. Wages are kept low while profits break records. Billionaires control newspapers and TV, buying up social media sites, refining their ideological machines to manipulate us under their hegemony. Infinite growth is demanded in a finite world.

Everything is competition – between companies, between workers, between states. Wars erupt over land and resources, we dehumanise each other and soldiers commit war crimes in the name of patriotism. Powerful nations invade and plunder smaller ones. Regimes send mercenaries and spies to crush people's uprisings against tyrants. The government spends whatever is needed to militarise the police, apparently to keep us safe from making a better world. There are wars on drugs and terrorism but no war on poverty – just wars against the poor.

In an era of social disintegration, monsters lurk. They blame the system's victims for the problems, not those with any power. Politicians and newspaper barons direct hate against immigrants, people on welfare or socialists: divide and rule – the oldest trick in the book. Islamophobia and antisemitism are all to evident. Violent, misogynistic incel ideology is commonplace online.[5] Neoliberalism accelerates this by destroying community cohesion. Reactionary conspiracy theories gain traction, sowing confusion and delusion. The scale of the crisis has allowed a dangerous politics of extremism to offer a persuasive vision of a return to the familiar, featuring strong nation states, rigid gender rules, and ignoring environmental concerns. The new far right groups are globally emboldened. The storming of the US Capitol in 2022 and the Brazilian Congress in 2023 showed the confidence of a movement driven to frenzy by claims of electoral fraud, burning with a passionate hatred of globalisation as a perceived attack on their national rights and power. Borders divide our planet and warp us as a species, filling our hearts with hate towards each other. These violent nationalist movements want to 'defend the borders', desperate to reverse the clock of progress to a make-believe time, rebuilding imagined ethno-nationalist communities. People with different skin tones, languages or religions are considered enemies while those who rule over us, exercising unimaginable power, laugh their way to the bank. The far right hate those whom they consider traitors to their vision, from liberals to communists. The bloodshed in Utøya and in Christchurch speaks to their growing violent rage and purpose. Misogynist YouTubers command loyal followers among young men around the world, and racist demagogues sell T-shirts while promoting the murder of demonstrators. They wage a war on 'woke' because they prefer an ignorant, sleeping world.

Who would have guessed that untrammelled capitalism was bad for humanity? Over the coming decades, the world is faced with the climate crisis and a return to authoritarian politics not seen for generations. To many people it seems as if the hopes for the future of rational, egalitarian politics have been robbed, stolen from us.

But we don't have to live like this.

Capitalism and its rotten ideologies have not always existed. Empires fall, and this one will, too. We can build a world without the incomprehensible dictates of the market, without the cruel indifferences of the directors and managers, without the unbearable sense everything is slipping away and we are powerless to stop it. We feel the urgency of the historic crisis. We cannot sit back and wait for capitalism to collapse – if it does it will be into a barbaric social breakdown not a better world. We need an alternative. This book is about that alternative, a vision of the future we could have. There is no excuse now for paralysis or demoralisation. There is everything to fight for. We know it will take time to build. Sometimes, it will be slow, then rush forward, and twenty years will happen in a day. But we can be ready, and prepared. There is a battle of the spirit *and* the flesh, a battle of ideas to decide the future.

Reclaim the Future

When we talk about reclaiming the future we mean this: that capitalism is not permanent and it can and must be replaced. Economic systems come and go – so too will the present order. Revolutions break out, social forces change and the basis of society is renewed. From the earliest days of industrial capitalism, over 200 years ago, there were already those who knew it could be replaced by something better. That we could take the best parts and create a world fit for all of us. Seize the capacities and productive forces of the modern age, over-throw the wretched minority that controls everything and begin to rationalise economics. Instead of everything being in private ownership, why not socialise the economy into the hands of the community, to be managed in a way that benefits everyone. These people were dismissed as utopian dreamers, and many of them were. But, as capitalism continued its relentless exploitation and revolutionary socialist ideas spread, it became clear that a challenge to capitalism could be posed. Not just the meagre piecemeal reforms of liberals, or changes to voting rights while people still slaved away for the profit of their masters, but something more profound.

One of the strategic problems for socialism today is the low political horizons of working people. When they don't have faith in themselves or their agency, they can be prey to reactionary populism or even fascist rhetoric. There has been a recent ideological offensive to propagate anti-intellectualism and ignorance, the notion that working people 'don't have time for all this nonsense'; in this way, the newspapers make out that working-class common sense is essentially Trumpism. Ridiculous lies.

We need an urgent focus on what the radical anthropologist David Graeber described as the basis of the left, the power of imagination, and the belief that 'the ultimate, hidden truth of the world is that it is something that we make, and could just as easily make differently. In this sense, a phrase like "all power to the imagination" expresses the very quintessence of the left'.[6] Discussions about the future are essential to free ourselves from the drudgery of the labour of Sisyphus of day-to-day campaigning with no end goal in sight.[7] We have to create time to speculate, wonder, imagine and hope. So, let's imagine how things might be different. No more markets, private capital, economic competition; no more nation states, no more rich or poor, in fact no more money. We can also think about Oscar Wilde's emphasis on the importance of a vision of the future; 'a map of the world that does not include Utopia is not worth even glancing at, for it leaves out the one country at which Humanity is always landing.' Here, we can understand Utopia – as Wilde does – not to as an impossible place but as a vision of a better place we strive for.

This book focuses on socialist democratic planning and popular democracy as a way to realign our global society within planetary boundaries and allow for our free development as conscious creative human beings. Only a socialist democratic plan will allow us to rationally organise our resources equitably. This is a radically new form of society, based on democratic forums that decide what and how to produce, what services to prioritise and when to use technology to reduce our working week, not make us unemployed. No more poverty alongside unimaginable wealth, no more hoarding while others starve.

This book advocates a future based on ecosocialism. Such a world will allow us to align human society with our talents and abilities, to master our destiny. It will not only bring humanity back into line with itself, freed from the imposed misery of scarcity, but bring us back into a rational relationship with the planet, healing the metabolic rift that has opened between people and nature that has deepened under capitalism. This is why we refer to *ecosocialism* as distinct from previous forms of social democracy or Stalinist regimes which had their own environmentally devastating impact. Ecosocialist democratic planning is about using technology and the latest productive techniques responsibly to provide everyone with a good life in a sustainable relationship to other life forms and the planet. It isn't that there would be no mistakes, but such mistakes could be democratically corrected by humans trying to consciously work out the best way to organise things rationally.

When Margaret Thatcher famously argued 'there was no alternative' to free-market capitalism, now we see the opposite is true. There is no alternative to ecosocialism as a way to rationalise the economy in line with planetary boundaries. Ecosocialism is the only possible future, but this doesn't mean it can happen *automatically*, without agency or thought. The contradictions of capitalism point in the direction of socialism as the only future – if the working class can overthrow the system. Rosa Luxemburg extended this to say that, in the face of global imperialist war, the options ahead were socialism or barbarism, the latter being what capitalism will bring about for society and the planet if it isn't overthrown.[8]

Reclaiming and popularising the ideas of ecosocialist democratic planning and participatory democracy is crucial to developing the kind of consciousness we need to actually overcome capitalism. We are at a disadvantage compared to the socialists of prior to the First World War because, in the eyes of billions, a form of socialism has not only been attempted but failed. We do not now have the luxury of being purposefully ambivalent or vague about a positive vision for a post-capitalist world.[9] We must be clear about how we can defeat capitalism as an economy based on plunder and exploitation in the interest of profit. Marxist philosopher István Mészáros argued against an aloof attitude to the question of the contours of the society that will replace capitalism because 'creating the necessary mediations towards [the abolition of capital] cannot be left to some far-away future … for if the mediatory steps are not pursued right from the outset, as an organic part of the transformatory strategy, they will never be taken'.[10] Sam Girdin, in *Catalyst Journal*, makes a passionate plea for 'establishing popular confidence in the feasibility of a socialist society'.[11]

As such this book is not afraid to draw heavily on the criticisms of our current blighted economy developed by Karl Marx in the 19th century. The argument of this book is that capital necessarily over-accumulates due to competition; it is exploitative of people and planet; it is wasteful due to over-production while also creating scarcity for millions; and it accelerates the gulf between humans and nature through all these processes. Marxism, as a revolutionary criticism of capitalism has the best framework to analyse and consider alternatives. However, this book maintains that the states that called themselves communist were not communist that in the sense that Marx or this book are talking about. To understand the difference is crucial to our survival as a species. Essentially, we need to free the idea of communism from the legacy of Stalinism.

What Is in This Book

This book is intended to help educate people who are becoming interested in socialism, and to contribute to more hopeful discussions about a future free from disaster capitalism. Its starting point is the idea that working people, from their different backgrounds, need to be aware of what socialism is and how it might operate. The political economy of socialism is *their* political economy.[12] A future world without class oppression is their future, that they will build. This might appear as 'utopian' (for now), but things move fast in dangerous times.

The ecological crisis has already led to a series of books that, by necessity, not only criticise capitalism but also explore alternatives.[13] These include the idea of nationalising Walmart, ecosocialist manifestos and speculative future fiction, such as *Half-Earth Socialism* or *Everything for Everyone: An Oral History of the New York Commune, 2052–2072* (both published in 2022), the latter firmly in the tradition of Edward Bellamy's Victorian socialist novel *Looking Backward* from 1888.[14] Two books have recently come out titled *Socialism or Extinction*, one by Martin Empson, another by Ted Reese.[15] In addition there is a plethora of books about post-capitalist degrowth economics as a response to ecological crisis, some liberal, some more radical, such as *Less is More* by Jason Hickel.[16] Futurology as advocated by people like Andy Hines is a growing industry.[17] There is new thinking on economics, such as *Doughnut Economics* by Kate Haworth or Tim Jackson's *Post-growth: Life after Capitalism*, Paul Mason's *Post-Capitalism* or Aaron Bastani's *Fully Automated Luxury Communism* were widely reviewed. *Utopia for Realists*, by Rutger Bregman (2015) – which advocated open borders, Universal Basic Income and a 15-hour working week – was a runaway bestseller, translated into over thirty languages. The list is growing as we scramble to find a way out.

This book is a contribution to the growing debate on post-capitalism. It is a synthesis of some of the historical debates over the nature of a transition from capitalism to socialism and then to a classless, stateless world of communism in which our humanity can genuinely flourish, free from social oppression and exploitation. But it is specifically focused also on ecosocialism as a way of considering the future. Ecosocialism is different from 'democratic socialism', as endorsed by some who believe in a gradual and legislative route to a better world. It is also different from the Stalinist command management model of Russia and Eastern Europe, or Socialism with Chinese Characteristics. The latter represents a reactionary nostalgia for a socio-political system a long way from human emancipation and the first is a modern-day 'greener capitalism' that leaves the heart of exploitation intact. Ecosocialism is also a long way away from the types of techno-utopianism, whereby automating work under capitalism leads inevitably towards socialism. At their core, these ideas advocate that modern capitalism will develop technologies to solve its contradictions and usher in a world of plenty without a revolutionary struggle. This is a technocratic socialism that emerges automatically from *within* capitalism's productive forces; all that is needed is a little political push to help them on the way.[18] We have to be cautious about imagining we can take the economics or technology of the present exploitative economic system and just 'make it socialist' – something more radical will be needed.

To be clear – this is not a dense economics textbook. To separate economics from politics or social issues is wrong (this is a problem with how mainstream economics is usually taught in universities). The book is a political argument for how we can organise post-capitalist society based on the self-activity of billions of people. This isn't an abstract vision; part of the debate is over the living, practical strategy to fight for such a world. This book starts from an outline of how capitalism functions familiar to socialist veterans (chapter 1) but necessary as the basis from which to develop an outline of a post-capitalist world. It also starts from the practical reality of our lives – we already have forms of planning within global private corporations, as well as experiences of the successes and failures of planning by different states. While it will take a revolution to shift power into the hands of the majority, we are not beginning from scratch (chapter 2). Chapter 3 outlines how a rationally planned economy might initially look and function.

The second part of this book is what you could consider supplementary material. You do not need to read these sections to understand the essential argument – but they will add context and wider perspectives. Of course every concept examined here is worthy of several books in themselves, this beginner's guide can only be an accessible summary. Because this book aims to make the rational case for a post-capitalist society it must also tackle the 'common-sense' arguments, for instance, whether humans are inherently greedy or if markets are 'natural'. There is also a short section examining the Russian socialist economy as 'look what happened in Russia' is an important argument to confront. There is a discussion on contemporary debates, whether we can rely on Big Data and algorithms, the role of AI and Universal Basic Income, as both are relevant to how we think of a socialist society. The final chapter is a culmination of the ecological thread running through the book about the debates on building a society that will meet human needs within planetary limits. This book is not the final answer to these questions but will provide the basis for you to enrich your ideas. As the historian Ronald Fraser said: 'go far beyond anything you've dreamt of, [or] read in books'.[19]

There are few times in history when the choice of roads is so clear. One leads to runaway global warming caused by capitalist exploitation and, potentially, to the death of billions as we collapse into barbarism. It means fascist governments as millions of climate refugees struggle to live; a world of slums, ingrained poverty and starvation as large parts of the planet become uninhabitable. Or a road towards a world of genuine democracy and a plan for our resources and work that heals the metabolic rift with nature and ends war, oppression and want forever.[20] The revolutionary and counter-revolutionary potential of global warming is apparent, the contradiction has to break one way or the other. This is what is at stake. This is why we must exert every ounce of energy to choose the correct road.

PART I

The Fight for an Ecosocialist Plan

1

How Does Capitalism Work?

The future is built from the accumulations of the past, but also from the ruptures and breaks in the present that open the possibilities of new directions. A socialist society will not be like a light switch suddenly turned on, it will be a struggle over many years to build, even after the capitalist class has been removed from power, and it will have to wrestle with the legacy of capitalism. As such, we must establish the basics of how capitalism functions to understand how socialist planning and workers' democracy is intended to replace the 'blind laws of the market'.

The prevailing view from defenders of the present economic system is that human society has always been *essentially* capitalist and this has always structured people's outlook of being selfish, individualistic and greedy. They point to the long-term existence of money and trade as evidence that our modern society is just a natural evolution of what happened before. This is pure ideology to justify the present state of things. In reality, human society has been organised in many different ways, with terrible violence and oppression being inflicted on people to secure the privileges and power of any given ruling class.

We once existed in simple Neolithic societies; people would hunt and gather fruits and vegetables and collectively raise children as needed. Society was relatively egalitarian as there was no time or resources for some people to separate themselves from the rest of the tribe. We were communal creatures who operated in groups; we had to collaborate to survive. What marked humans out from other animals was our ability to imagine, which led to art and symbolic culture. The cave paintings of our ancestors were part of the same process of reflection and critical thinking that allowed us to create civilisation. Even in Neolithic times we had buildings like those found at Göbekli Tepe, in modern-day Turkey, constructed by hunter gatherers two thousand years before any humans learned to read or write, or began to formalise architecture.

When we developed tools and began to use animals for farming, we revolutionised our society and our relationship to the Earth. It wasn't just that we started to use tools – some other primates use simple tools too – it was that we learned how to *standardise* them and shared that information with each other. We didn't just pick up a rock to use as a hammer, we perfected the hammer as a design. It existed in our imagination. As tools and techniques developed, we produced a surplus food. This surplus allowed a division of labour because we could form more complex social arrangements if everyone did not need to spend their time foraging or hunting. People could develop as artisans, builders, or administrators allowing them to construct towns and cities. It also created class divisions. The surplus was claimed by people (usually men) who remodelled themselves as emperors or kings and ruled states defended by soldiers. Priests and seers emerged to foster ideology to support these regimes and to create an educated bureaucracy to help regulate the distribution of the surplus through laws and moral codes. Human history as we know it is primarily (although not exclusively) driven by the social evolution, and occasional revolution, of different ways of exploiting the mass of people for the benefit of a minority.

From the development of these first early types of societies, humanity has constantly revolutionised its economics
and developed new methods.[1] Huge ancient empires like
those of the Greeks and the Romans were built on the backs
of slaves. During the Middle Ages in Europe, if you were a
peasant, you had a piece of land to provide your subsistence,
but you also worked a few days a week for the local lord or
baron on their land. You would not have to rely on selling
your crops for money to purchase food. You might sell any
excess that you had, but you had your own means of production – your field, cow, and goat. But all or most of the surplus
went to the local lord. This was justified in religious terms,
that told people to know their place because the social order
was divinely ordained. Nevertheless, people would still resist
and peasant revolts took place that rocked medieval Europe.

Early capitalism emerged in the English countryside, with
landowners making money producing crops or wool to sell to
the cities.[2] Within this society a class of merchants enriched
themselves through commerce. As trade develops the amount
of credit and money expands, and begins to take the form
of capital, seeking out ways to invest. Enterprising merchants
seeking to put this money to work realised that instead of
buying cheap and selling dear, why not build the things to
be sold? They began investing in production, for which they
needed cheap labourers. Where to find them? Through controlling parliament they passed laws to forcibly evict peasants
from their land – leaving them with no means of survival but
selling their ability to work. This created the modern working
class in England, the first country where capitalism emerged.
In the colonies across the Americas the need for labour was
so great for growing crops that the colonial masters sought
out slaves from Africa, justifying this barbaric practice with a
racist ideology.

It was this initial act of violence and expropriation against the masses that marked the beginning of the tyranny of capital. Torn away from any means to sustain ourselves, all we have is our ability to work, which we must sell to someone in return for wages. This economic relationship is presented to us as one of apparently equal parties – a boss and labourer, employer and employee, capitalist and worker. Our exploitation is hidden from us, obscured by the lie that we are somehow equal, that you do a fair day's work a fair day's pay.

Capital was put to work by the middle classes, small producers and artisans in the cities and large towns across Europe to make them richer. Capital came to increasingly dominate agriculture in England during the 18th century as money was invested to make more money.[3] But those with capital did not have power, landed aristocracies and kings (and occasionally queens) had power. What the early bourgeoisie desired was power to allow them to create a world that would realise *their* true potential. This is what the political and social revolutions from 1789 onwards were about, overthrowing the old feudal rulers so that capital could dominate the economy. This was the birth of capital*ism* as a system of political rule.[4]

What Is Capital(ism)?

Today, capital dominates the world. On a superficial level, capital is just large sums of money – money that is invested to make more money. The capitalists portray themselves as merely lucky – wealthy people with good business sense. Of course, their money is itself the product of centuries of class division, struggle, war, exploitation and misery. It is the accumulation of the surplus produced by previous generations that has been transformed into money and wealth. Capital takes over, it co-opts and integrates.

Capital is more than money; it is a *social relationship*. Someone with capital can hire someone to work for them. There are those with capital who invest and those without capital who work.[5] When socialists talk about capital it is not just money, it is a way of organising the economy and all the required forms of social control, coercion, and laws. It is a totality – it is so pervasive it spreads across the world, moulding politics and society to its needs. Even science, supposedly objective, is bent to the will of the ruling ideologies.[6] Laws govern contracts and commerce more than anything else – property is nine tenths of the law after all. Everywhere around us we can see capital as a social relationship based on a metabolism of social control; the dictates and demands of capital on us as humans and on the planet are tyrannical. To better control us, capital also created the modern nation state as feudal kingdoms broke down and nationalism emerged as a dominant ideology, binding working people to their bosses through the notion of a shared community.[7] It also hides behind concepts such as 'liberty, democracy, free society, free enterprise, and open society' to mask the dictatorship of capital over our lives.[8]

Capital is used to buy workshops, factories, offices, equipment, plants (the means of production) and workers to create commodities or provide a service, which are then sold on the market for a profit. This is why capitalist economics is such a complex (dis)functional system; it has many capitals, each operating autonomously, while also integrated and warring against each other in the marketplace.

Capital creates a system of mass commodity production in which the means of production are privately owned by the capitalist class, or, occasionally, by the capitalist state acting on their behalf. The capitalists make money by paying workers to produce commodities and provide services – everything has a use value but also an *exchange* value. It must be sold to make profit.

Competition forces capital to inexorably accumulate and grow or it will face bankruptcy, hostile takeovers, or eventually perish. It does not care about what is good for people or planet. It takes all the genuine work that needs to be done by humans (healthcare, teaching, sports, cleaning, entertainment, furniture making, etc.) and turns everything into a commodity to be exchanged. This is why capital cannot be 'ethical' – as an economic regulator all it can do is strive for profit. If something is not profitable then it is not useful for investors. This means it cannot rationally distribute or allocate what is *needed* for humanity. A good example is food – we already produce enough to feed everyone globally, but around 850 million still suffer from insufficient daily nutrition. Capital will never just provide the food where it is needed. The need for profit and return on investment means that food is hoarded or wasted (becoming spoilt) to protect market prices.

The hard economic logic of capital was demonstrated in an infamous 1992 World Bank internal memo signed by the then President Larry Summers, which calculated the economic benefits of exporting pollution to poorer countries in the global South. It argued that 'under-populated countries in Africa are vastly under-polluted' and stated: 'I think the economic logic behind dumping a load of toxic waste in the lowest wage country is impeccable.'[9] *The Economist* magazine backed the memo, arguing that anything that slows down economic growth would only create poverty; 'If clean growth means slower growth, as it sometimes will, its human cost will be lives blighted by a poverty that would otherwise have been mitigated.'[10]

Capital introduced a level of competition and economic power that did not exist previously. It developed the forces of production (machinery, equipment, power, etc.) through industrialisation never before seen levels. Its division of labour has boosted the productivity of humans to levels never dreamt of, lifting millions out of poverty and increasing the standards of living for many people. This is why Karl Marx and Friedrich Engels applauded the revolutionary early period of capitalism, when it tore down the old decayed systems and built a new dynamic society that could finally meet human needs.[11]

But no matter how beneficial capitalism might appear, it prevents us achieving our full potential because these potentials are controlled and dominated by the capital owned by a small number of people, and because capitalism is based on the demand for profit and accumulation. It has grown at great cost to the planet and has given people a life that is nothing compared to what they could have had if the profits and power were not concentrated in the hands of the capitalist class.

Capitalism has evolved over its lifetime. Many countries introduced universal suffrage, with greater access to welfare, healthcare and education. As the working class became more organised, the capitalists were forced to make concessions: holiday pay, the weekend as free time, and maternity and paternity rights were all granted. The fight for sustainable social reproduction and against immiseration brought about comprehensive education, healthcare, an expansion of local government to cover the needs of elderly and disabled people, in short, a public sector or a social wage – paid for through general taxation – to make life bearable. After the Second World War, Western capitalism went through various phases: the New Deal, the managerial revolution, monetarism, neoliberalism and so on. The types of work evolved, but one thing remained fundamental – the subordination of labour to capital.[12]

Under capitalism there is not just the capitalist class and the working class (or the myriad types of professional, self-employed or middle-class people) – there is also an older form of exploitation that pre-dates our current economy but also thrives in it – landlords and rentiers. These are people who make money from owning something and leasing or renting it to you. A classic example is housing, but many different types of assets can be turned into economic rent, especially digital technologies. For instance, increasingly you cannot buy software packages, you have to license software from the company that made it, increasing their profits as they can charge a regular amount. Rentiers exploit humans just as much as, though differently from, the capitalist class, and not just working-class people. Anyone who needs housing and has to rent can end up paying exorbitant costs towards simply having a home, even though, according to the United Nations (UN) housing is one of the basic human rights.

How Does Capital Organise Work?

Those who have power have always looked upon the rest of us as mere units of production to create wealth for them. The principle of work is expressed in Genesis 3:19: 'By the sweat of your face you shall eat bread, till you return to the ground, for out of it you were taken; for you are dust, and to dust you shall return.' We are human dust to them, we emerge, we are exploited, we 'deserve bread' only because we need it to sustain ourselves, and then we return to dust, to be replaced by the next generation. Such is the life of working people through the ages.

But under capitalism the nature of work begins to change. The shift from peasant life – where you owned your own means of production in the form of land and maybe some livestock – to waged labour marks the emergence of the modern working class. With no other means to sustain themselves, people were forced into dangerous work in factories and associated industries and labour, working more than 12-hour days to earn their wages to survive. Child labour was routine, the capitalists even boasted about how 'We have introduced certain methods of diversion for the children. We teach them to sing during their work, also to count while working.'[13] Life was nasty brutish and short; thankfully, workers were easily replaceable.

Capital's revolutionary break with previous economic systems was not just the development of new technologies like steam power or the combustion engine but the way that work was completely reorganised. No longer were we primarily agricultural workers; people were moved from fields to small cottage industries, into workshops, and then into factories and offices – huge workplaces employing hundreds of people. Thousands of people worked in steel factories or across retail and transport. The creation of a huge working class was the material basis for modern capitalism, and capital ruthlessly regiments labour, dividing up the work, reorganising people's lives and putting humans under the control of machinery so as to maximise profit. Capital starts from the cooperative, social nature of work and fuses this with the forces of production to create a system of mass commodity production. This is the social division of labour. It is also the domination of capital, which demands to be the master, to determine the social metabolism of our lives with each other and with nature.[14]

The introduction of new machinery and technology to speed up efficiencies is, for many workers, a profoundly alienating experience, 'condemning the workers to increasing alienation, economic insecurity, and cognitive degradation'.[15] It deepens the split between manual and intellectual work, between the technical-managerial sections of the working class and those reduced to simpler and simpler tasks. The main benefit of the introduction of new technology and machinery is that it increases the subsumption of labour to capital and gives the capitalists an excuse to make workers redundant, creating unemployment, which is used to drive down wages.[16]

Your wages are the cost of your labour power as a commodity, that is, the price of what it takes to keep you alive in terms of food and rent/mortgage at the cultural and social level you would expect. Some workers can command higher prices for their labour power because they have more advanced educational qualifications or technical skills, but this is only a small, relatively privileged layer of workers. Under capitalism, the myth is that workers and capitalists are equals – one exchanges their time and efforts for a 'fair wage'. For socialists there is no fair wage under capitalism, you are exploited by the capitalist class to make money for them.[17]

The transformation of people into units of labour power turned them into a commodity like any other – no different from a wrench or a loom, or a computer or a tonne of steel. Workers are just a commodity to be put into the production process, driven to exhaustion, exposed to unsafe conditions, injured at work, or driven to the point where their bodies break down before their time – all in service of the bosses' permanent economic war against their rivals. Even the early theorist of capitalism Adam Smith admitted that work was a source of 'toil and trouble … of our own bodies'.

Another crucial aspect of the social division of labour is the difference between mental and physical labour, between conception and execution. The working class is not just factory workers. Capitalism certainly requires 'blue collar' manual jobs to make and move things, but it also needs workers to organise the economy. Managers, technicians, lawyers and other specialisms ensure the wheels of production and distribution turn smoothly. Once we understand the social division of labour, and how expansive the number of roles essential to capital, we can see that the working class has not shrunk, as some claim, but in fact has grown massively across the world. Modern capital requires increasingly complex forms of value production, more technical divisions of labour, an expansive managerial class, armies of workers in logistics, distribution, ICT support and so on. Factory work also hasn't gone away; industrial work has just shifted to different parts of the world.

This social division of labour is also a key battleground for gender and race. Capital integrates the pre-existing hierarchies among people and creates new forms of them. For instance, historically, women were expected to maintain families, to raise children, clean homes and so on. Capital reinforced this gendered division of labour, relying increasingly on free domestic labour to sustain exploitation of workers elsewhere. Even after decades of feminism, women still do more housework than men. Capital ignores this type of labour, focusing only on the capitalist category of waged labour, because that is where profit can be made. The jobs that many women do are often seen as extensions of their 'natural role' in the family, as cleaners, teachers, cooks, secretaries, and personal assistants. When women do have careers, they can end up taking months or years off work to raise children, because it is assumed that they will do it rather than their male partners. The gender dynamic cuts through capitalism because the nuclear family is an essential part of social reproduction for the benefit of capital. As a result women, particularly those in underdeveloped countries, have been excluded from the 'free market'.

Likewise with race. Discrimination and prejudice on the part of mostly white management structures relegate Black and Asian people to 'ethnic jobs'. They are then more likely to face being disciplined at work, to be paid less money and so on. Capital is racialised over what jobs it provides and what kind of pay people get. The division of labour is often a racist division. The colour line of jobs is a global one; capital structures economic activity across borders and consigns people to extractive work, or semi-skilled work across the global South. Majority black countries are used as dumping grounds for rubbish from the global North and underdevelopment means they are unattractive for investment.

Between the big capitalists and the working class is a whole layer of people who might own small businesses or see themselves as 'professionals'. They are the middle classes, often in an antagonistic relationship towards capital and labour, sometimes occupying both roles at the same time. The middle classes are confronted by the power of big capital and struggle to compete with it (think of a small corner shop next to a giant supermarket). Where they hire workers, they are compelled to pay lower wages with fewer benefits because they lack the revenue to compete with larger companies. Despite the capitalist propaganda that exalts entrepreneurs and self-made businesspeople, most small businesses fail, leaving people in debt and depressed. According to the US government, around 20 per cent of small businesses fail in the first year, more than 50 per cent fail in the first five years and, after a decade, only 30 per cent are still active, though how many of them are profitable is unclear.[18]

Without capital and relying on their wages to survive, workers have established trade unions to resist. Trade unions have been repeatedly banned, delegitimised, straitjacketed and legislated against to within an inch of their life in capitalist countries because they point to an inescapable truth about work under capital – that there is an inherent antagonism between bosses and workers, and workers are stronger when they overcome their atomisation and struggle together.

It is the unequal position between workers and their employers that underscores socialist politics, and why the working class features so strongly as the class that will be able to change the world and win the future. A fundamental point of socialist politics that any worker can understand is that capitalism is a system of not just contradictions but also antagonisms. The workplace is a site of struggle because workers are exploited. The boss is not elected, but appointed to manage, to control, to decide. Bosses can berate you, discipline you, sack you if they want. Capitalism is a system of disequilibrium, of oppression and resistance, ruptures and repression.

Surplus Value

Every society is really determined by how it produces a surplus beyond immediate sustenance and what it does with that surplus. One key argument socialists make that is different from 'mainstream' economics is that profits do not come from the market exchange of goods or services. That is only where the profits are *realised*. Profits come from the labour process, from workers' efforts to make commodities, provide a service, facilitate transportation and so on. Under capitalism in the production of any commodity, the capitalist needs the factory or workplace with all its tools and equipment alongside workers to do the work. Wages are set high enough to reproduce a worker's labour power, to pay for the things we need to get us back to work the next day, including sustenance and social time according to our status – workers in finance earn a lot more than a cleaner because their labour is seen as more valuable to the capitalist class. But we are not paid the full value of our labour. Workers produce a surplus above the value of their wages – it is this surplus that is turned into profit by the capitalist class. The service you provide or the things you make return more money to the business than their costs in wages or other overheads (otherwise the business goes bankrupt). The easiest ways to boost profit are either to increase prices or to produce more for less. To do so you can extend the working day or cut back on breaks (this increases the *absolute* surplus value). Alternatively, businesses can invest in new technology to produce things more efficiently (increasing the *relative* surplus value).[19]

Imagine you are serving drinks in a cafe for a multinational coffee company. You do not see a Starbucks with 20 staff members; the company understands the most efficient ratio of staff working time and hourly pay to provide the expected service. The company has expectations on how fast you can perform your job based on the average amount of time it takes for all employees.

So how does the market work? Any good or service has a usefulness, its *use* value. Water and basic foods probably have the highest use value of all (alongside oxygen) and yet they are mostly quite cheap (or free). Yet a diamond has very little use value (unless you want to make a drill) but costs a lot of money. This is because the price of any given good or service is based on its *exchange* value, not its *use* value. The *exchange* value is not worked out by the exertions or efforts of an individual worker, it is worked out by the *socially necessary labour time* that goes into any and all types of commodities.[20] The thing that determines the ultimate value of commodities is not the concrete work of any person or group of people, but the combined total of all work done by all people that then has to be exchanged on the market to make a profit. This is the subordination of *concrete* labour to *abstract* labour, and the supremacy of the law of value. It mediates all of our lives and social relations with each other. It is the defeat of actual humans and the triumph of 'economics' as something beyond us and out of our control.

Exchange value exists because an item is scarce, or rather it is not abundant. If something is abundant it is hard to put a price on it and even harder to make a profit out of it. Commodities under capitalism have their specific values because there is not enough for everyone – often because capitalists control what is made available for sale. Milk and butter should be free (at least in Europe) because it is so over-produced by farmers that they end up destroying tonnes of produce to avoid flooding the market and causes prices to collapse.[21]

We can see a real-life example of the relationship between labour and profit. In July 2021 the owner of Heavenly Pizza in Ohio gave his staff all the takings for one day to show employee appreciation. The staff's wages went up from what we can assume is close to the minimum wage to $78 an hour.[22] The staff were reportedly grateful, calling it a gift and expressing their appreciation for such a kind act from their benevolent boss. What this exercise showed was the actual *value* of their labour. The takings from the pizzeria totalled $6,300 – normally the manager would have deducted the wages from that and then the remaining money is surplus value, which would go towards buying more pizza ingredients, the overheads for the shop and of course profit. Those workers got a glimpse of what their labour power was worth to the boss. People in some jobs, like lawyers in firms, already know the difference between their wage and their value because they submit billable hours to clients. But for most workers it is obscured by the labour process and the erroneous concept of 'a fair day's pay for a fair day's work'.

Now the question is clear: can we reorganise society so we control what happens to the surplus and where it goes?

The Law of Value

We have seen how capital exploits labour, but how does capitalism work as a functioning system? The driving force of the capitalist production method can be summed up as the law of value – it is this law that determines whether businesses will succeed or fail. So, let's explain the law of value so we can understand what changes need to be made.

A lot of economic textbooks focus on isolated examples, or how only one person's economic activity occurs. Under capitalism we are not talking about small workshops with carpenters or blacksmiths making a handful of goods a week, as existed in the Middle Ages. Capitalism is a complex global totality in which, every day, billions of workers engage in every kind of economic activity. So how do we measure the value that is made? For instance, how do we compare different types of labour for wages? Building a fighter jet or a school? Printing a book or chopping down a tree?

Let's return to the barista in the last section. That was an example of *concrete* specific labour – someone harvests coffee beans, someone transports those beans to a warehouse, someone makes a frappuccino and sells it to a customer. This is concrete work, but capital can only be invested by following laws of economic motion that generate a profit. It has to calculate decisions based on the socially necessary labour time that goes into any operation. Your work exists within a society in which all work is congealed together and then averaged out, this is the *abstract* labour, the basis of economic life for capital.[23]

It is abstract because it refers to waged labour in general, not the specifics of any one job in any one place. Goods and services must be stamped with a quantitative amount (money) through the act of labour, but the work done is different. An airline pilot is working when they fly a plane, but how do you compare their work to that of a deep-sea oil rig worker or someone cleaning toilets? Things have exchange value 'only because human labour in the abstract has been embodied or materialised in it'.[24] The unique model of working under capitalism is the way labour, all work, is wrapped up into a social whole. All the commodities produced are created by workers across businesses, factories and workshops around the world – all producing value that is translated into profit by the capitalists when it is exchanged on the market. And just as abstract labour exists, so too does abstract capital once we talk about capital as a totality and not specific capitals.[25]

The result of producing in this way is that society is dominated by the *law of value*, the generalised exchange of *all* commodities according to the quantity of socially necessary abstract labour time used to make them. It coordinates commodity production by ensuring that socially necessary labour time determines the value of everything and that 'extraction of surplus labour is subjected to the maximisation of exchange value'.[26] This is the myriad billions of economic calculations and actions that happen all the time throughout the economy that determine the value of what we make and the services we provide.[27] The law of value governs the capitalist economy because production and investment are guided by effective demand from consumers.[28] It is how capitalists decide where to hire people and what work they should do. The law of value is unique and essential to capitalism.

While capitalism cannot measure or even understand this social calculation, it goes on every day; any good manager has an intuition for how many workers should be assigned to a task and on what kind of wages. Any company must work out a price and it does so by taking all the input costs (wages, materials, wear and tear, transportation, marketing, etc.) and adding an average profit rate. That gives you your price for the market. Get the price wrong and you will sell below exchange value and lose money. Get it too high and you'll be undercut by the competition and all that value will sit in warehouses and go to waste, unrealised.

This is where the law of value is essential in capitalism – it helps regulate the economy across different sectors of capital. It is only through comparing the value of commodities and services produced by all of us in the social economy that we can adequately compare different labour in different industries. As one economist described it, 'Value is the transmission belt which transfers the movement of working processes from one part of society to another, making that society a functioning whole.'[29]

Speeding up production, making workers work faster, more efficiently, doing the same amount of work with fewer people, all of these are crucial for profitability. Time is the whip of capital, it is the logic of domination. It is why, from the beginning of capitalism, workers have fought bosses over the length of the working day, or slowing work down, or for longer breaks, more holidays, and bosses respond by trying to increase productivity, speed up production, and demand longer hours. This is what Marx meant when he wrote that 'time is everything, man is nothing; he is, at most, time's carcass. Quality no longer matters. Quantity decides everything; hour for hour, day by day.'[30]

It is worth noting that the average European peasant had a far shorter working week than a modern worker. It was with the advent of capitalism that spending a third of your entire life engaged in work was normalised.[31] This struggle over time was also the basis of trade unionism; workers fought over the allocation of time and the rate of exploitation – hence the campaign for the eight-hour day.

Modern capitalism has recently used technological innovations to capture value rather than make it. Modern tech companies like Uber, Airbnb and others add nothing of productive value to the economy, instead they create interfaces between consumers and workers (or landlords), essentially making money from rent instead of selling (or owning) anything. This has been labelled a new form of techno-feudalism, though in many ways it is just the latest version of parasitic grifting by corporations that are adding nothing of value while getting rich. Huge legal battles about intellectual property dominate court rooms as corporations deploy lawyers to fiercely guard the ideas and symbols that generate profit.

What helps the capitalists is that the law of value is incredibly efficient and useful *if* you are producing surplus value for profit. When economists talk about market efficiencies, they are saying that the law of value is the dominant economic regulator and is forcing a certain intensity of work that is 'efficient', and that prices can be set at a level that makes money for investors. But the law of value can be in contradiction to society's needs – just because it is a good regulator of the socially necessary labour time needed to produce something and make a profit does not mean it is good at allocating what people *need*. The law of value cannot produce a balanced and optimal division of labour beyond what is good for the exchange value of commodities. It must be overcome through socialist democratic planning.

What is Money? And What about 'Commodity Fetishism'?

A lot of anti-capitalists believe that the 'love of money is the root of all evil'. Arguing that corporate greed and capitalist enrichment exist while millions struggle to survive is an important *moral* argument for socialism, but money itself is not particularly important in terms of overthrowing capitalist society. Certainly, people who focus on abolishing money as the primary and initial task of socialism are putting the cart before the horse.

Money functions as a *universal commodity-equivalent*. It is a commodity like any other, but we use it to trade for things we want on a general basis. It is much more efficient than bartering, where you might not have a thing to exchange that is wanted by the person you are trying to get something from (you have wool to give them in exchange for wood, but they don't want any wool). As such, money is a universal commodity-equivalent that is essential if exchange value is the dominant form of social interaction between commodities; 'it is impossible to abolish money itself as long as exchange value remains the social form of products'.[32] Money is the *mediation* of the labour invested in each good or service and is a way of easily gauging the exchange value of a thing between industries.

Money is representative of the relational value between humans and what they are making or doing in terms of economic activity, and the value that society gives something (which under capitalism is distorted by profit, market economics and so on). This is what Marx means when he writes 'money is not a thing, it is a social relation'.[33] Money also has a second function as a unit of accounting. It creates a universally understood measure of value that can be tracked, regulated and traded. It is also essential to understanding the relationship between credit and debt. It is this function that socialists are particularly interested in when we think about a post-capitalist world.

Money is a good way to talk about the problem of commodity fetishism. One of the problems of a capitalist society is that we do not consider our labour in relation to other workers. We feel atomised. We might identify with our immediate work-mates or others in our industry, but we do not see how we relate to each other as a social whole. Basically, whenever we go to the shops, we do not value any of the things we want to buy in terms of human labour, we do not understand or see how our labour is connected to everyone else's through the medium of money (the universal commodity-equivalent). Our society hides the social character of our work and the social relations between us as individual workers, by making our relations appear as relations *between* material objects.[34] This is commodity fetishism, and it obscures the reality of capital.

This is a process which starts with reification, a process that converts social relations between people into *things*. We see commodities and their prices all around us, and not the reality of the wage relation of capital and labour and the social basis of capitalism. We might toil in a big workplace alongside others, but when we interact with the products and services of other workers, the relation is mediated because it happens through purchasing things as commodities. Reification makes the alienation of how we interact with commodities appear entirely natural and normal.

Moreover, in a competitive economy where we interact through the medium of the market, the possession of things becomes important to us; they condition and ultimately determine our worth and role in the world. We *fear* scarcity and poverty, and it conditions our sense of self worth. At its most extreme end, this is the fetishism around sports cars, Rolex watches, gold jewellery, because these things are presented in the market as amazing, wonderful possessions based on abstracted exchange value, not their use values. Put simply, commodity fetishism treats value as a *property* of things and not the *social relations* that have made them.

The important thing about this concept is that it explains the power of the ideology of capitalism. We are not dealing simply with a conspiracy of the rich propped up by right-wing journalism – if ideology was this shallow then we would have overthrown the system by now. It also is not the case that people are 'idiots' who don't understand what is going on; we live in a nexus of overlapping and self-reinforcing power–property–legal–philosophical and religious ideologies rooted in the very way society is organised. The rule of capital is obscured by the way it organises society. Fetishistic thinking about capital is rooted in our existence as workers who contribute to the social product of society only through the individual basis of our actions.[35] We appear to live in a world of fair and equal exchange – you work and in exchange you get paid. We all see 'capital's logic as self-evident natural laws'.[36] The idea that capitalism, that market exchange as the way to organise the economy, is somehow normal and has always been with us delegitimises alternatives and shuts down dissent. This is the idea of bourgeois hegemony; the ruling ideas of any time are the ideas of its ruling class.[37] Attempts to overthrow or circumvent the 'natural order' of capitalism are denounced and sometimes violently broken up by the state acting on behalf of the capitalist class.

This vast, complex society we have built confronts us as something alien, something acting against our interests, somehow *beyond* us. This thing called the 'economy' determines our lives, the billions of economic calculations and decisions made everyday by something called 'the market'. For example, the tenant farmers in John Steinbeck's *Grapes of Wrath* faced by the men from the bank foreclosing on them, argue:

'Sure,' cried the tenant men, 'but it's our land.... We were born on it, and we got killed on it, died on it. Even if it's no good, it's still ours.... That's what makes ownership, not a paper with numbers on it.'

'We're sorry. It's not us. It's the monster. The bank isn't like a man.'

'Yes, but the bank is only made of men.'

'No, you're wrong there – quite wrong there. The bank is something else than men. It happens that every man in a bank hates what the bank does, and yet the bank does it. The bank is something more than men, I tell you. It's the monster. Men made it, but they can't control it.'

Capitalism is that monster. We made it, but we cannot control it. Whenever we try to tame it, those in power claim it is beyond our control – 'market forces'. If we organise against it, they send in their police or strike-breakers to beat us down.

How to strip away the fetishism and the ideology that surrounds it? It is not easy, but Marx argues that we can do so from a perspective of understanding how things were different in the past (in pre-capitalist societies), so we can explain how they changed, but also crucially 'points which indicate the transcendence of the present form of production relations, the movement coming into being, thus *foreshadowing* the future ... for a new state of society'.[38] One of the benefits of socialism, as a conscious plan of the economy, is that we will begin to understand the nature of what is produced and its worth. We will no longer live in a world of commodities and an invisible 'economy' with baffling laws and terrible consequences. Commodity fetishism will wither away as we grasp what the true value of everything is and restore our humanity in the face of the dire inversions of reality that capital faces us with.

Scarcity is Our Mode of Life

How has capitalism conditioned us? It is not just about competition as a good – as we mentioned earlier, it is about fear of scarcity. Capital creates scarcity, and landlords and rentiers exploit it. Simon Sutterlütti and Stefan Meretz explain, 'Today our needs are formed under conditions of exclusion. This creates a strong need for security, as a reaction to the constant worry of being excluded and losing freedoms.'[39] Security breeds a flourishing human being, scarcity breeds the opposite. This is the essential bedrock of reactionary thinking and therefore the basis for the psychological continuation of capitalism even when it is manifestly destructive. It is the material structural basis for racism and nationalism, two of the most powerful ideologies of the modern age. Ironically, while capital is predicated on scarcity, with most people having very few or only narrow options, capital is routinely *over-producing*.[40]

Scarcity is how the politicians justify pro-capitalist policies. The 2008 financial crisis led to a wave of austerity, as governments argued that a crisis in the banking sector had to lead to public sector cuts and wage freezes. In fact, austerity has been a pretty common feature of the capitalist system in many countries since the oil crisis of 1973, an excuse for capitalists to restructure economies to suit their interests. As Jason Hickel explains in *Less is More*:

Since the 1980s endless waves of privatisation have been unleashed all over the world, of education, healthcare, transport, libraries, parks, swimming pools, water, housing, even social security. Social goods everywhere are under attack for the sake of growth. The idea is that by making public goods scarce, people will have no choice but to purchase private alternatives.[41]

The politics of scarcity is the basis of global relations as well, 'The condition for prosperity, growth and rising average living standards in a particular zone of capitalist economic activity becomes the failure of other zones to adequately compete and thereby prevent a transfer of value to more competitive zones.'[42] We see this in the anguish of workers in the Western nations as they see their jobs moved abroad to the global South where labour costs are cheaper. It is in the faces of workers who cross picket lines, too scared to lose a day's pay to fight for a better wage in the future. Countries that are ostensibly richer, like Switzerland or Sweden, have mass racist parties on the basis of protecting their relative privilege in the global order.

The consequences of scarcity can be seen in the fury of the far right, whipping up race hate against immigrants for 'taking' jobs and housing. The existence of scarcity breeds nationalism and racism, it immiserates and destroys. Since 2008, the global economy has become weaker, less able or willing to provide for the mass of people. Young people today have a worse living standard than their parents in most countries. The feeling that globalisation and neoliberalism has made life more insecure – moved jobs abroad, lowered wages, brought in more migrants – is a core anxiety for many people. They become susceptible to right-wing ideology: close the borders, protect your own, build a strong state and powerful nation, cut back on foreign aid. Scarcity is at the root of this reactionary thinking.

This ideological structure in the modern age is seized upon by online grifters, a huge and growing industry, encouraging people to set up small businesses and use automation and online tech to get rich quick. Books like *The 4-hour Workweek:*

Escape 9–5, Live Anywhere, and Join the New Rich, by Tim Ferris, pioneered encouraging people to escape the rat race of exploited wage labour by setting up an online business, exploiting super-exploited labour in the global South and then sitting back to watch the money roll in. The ideological structure creates a culture where people don't look to collective action and solidarity to change things for the better but just to become 'mini-capitalists', replicating the same pathological human relations that people are trying to escape from.

Because capitalism can even exploit misery as a business, the long hours worked in modern capitalist societies (a scarcity of *time*) create the conditions for new industries to emerge to assist with the social reproduction of exhausted workers with little free time: paid care for the young and elderly, medication for sleep and depression, counselling and so on.[43]

But scarcity also creates the conditions for potential social revolution. 'Demand exceeds supply; those who Have use the idea of private property and the coercive power of the state to reinforce their position; those who Have Not compete for the social product with every means at their disposal from beggary to revolution.'[44] Scarcity is central to inequality and is understood as a powerful tool for maintaining capitalism. Boris Johnson, at the time Mayor of London, stated clearly in a speech that 'some measure of inequality is essential for the spirit of envy and keeping up with the Joneses that is, like greed, a valuable spur to economic activity'.[45] This points to the importance of socialists advocating for a society that provides security for people by fighting to overcome scarcity.

Capitalist Crises are Social Crises

Supporters of capitalism point to what a wonderful system it is: raising living standards and creating technologies previously undreamed of. It would be wrong to deny the reality of how capital and capitalism have created incredible dynamics of growth and fundamentally transformed the world for the better considering what came before. But it is equally undeniable that capital is an economic force that is crisis prone and subject to recessions and depressions; '[c]rises are a feature of capitalism, not a bug'.[46]

Earlier, we looked at the environmental crisis caused by capital. Now we must outline how the drive for profitability necessitates capital accumulation that creates regular crises. Unlike previous human societies, where a social and economic crisis would be caused by something like a drought or plague, capitalist economic crises are caused by capital being *too* successful. Writing in 1848, Marx and Engels outlined the basic problem:

In these crises, there breaks out an epidemic that in all earlier epochs would have seemed an absurdity – the epidemic of overproduction ... industry and commerce seem to be destroyed; and why? Because there is too much civilisation, too much means of subsistence, too much industry, too much commerce.[47]

In pre-capitalist societies supply and demand were pretty equal, in that small-scale production meant people made things to order (you wanted horseshoes or a new tunic or a hammer and it was made for you). The use value of things was more obvious and related to the price more than the abstract exchange value we have under capitalism.[48] There was no capability to mass produce in the way factories do – Britain's first factory was in Derby in 1721, the first factory in the USA was only opened in 1793.

The competition hardwired into capitalism is both its strength (in terms of economic dynamism) and the cause of crises. Different capitals are at economic war for market share, they must accumulate, grow and consolidate as they chase profits. Investors, hungry for dividends, and rival firms innovate with new products or labour-saving techniques of production. New technology is required, more machines and more power to make more products or provide services faster – with fewer workers, if possible. The more that is produced, the more demand is made for raw materials, and the economy expands. This eventually leads to a crisis of over-production ('too much commerce, too much civilisation') and goods can no longer be sold profitably. A crisis of profitability hits major companies causing panic among investors and boards of directors. They lay off staff and close plants and factories, destroying capital. This exacerbates a wider social crisis that cascades the problem; unemployed people generally buy less. A recession grips the economy.

There are many countervailing tendencies to this breakdown of capitalist profitability which help to lessen the inevitable problems of over-accumulated capital. Cutting wages, increasing productivity, or even moving jobs abroad to take advantage of cheaper labour can all temporarily offset the declining rate of profit, but eventually a bust will aways follow a boom. Credit is a very important factor in lubricating the wheels of capital and commerce, though even that can lead to bigger problems further into the business cycle if over-extended businesses start to default on loans.

The crisis itself helps resolve the problem of profitability, because bankrupt capitalists sell their assets and other sectors of capital can buy it up cheap, boosting their profits.[49] When discussing crisis there is a tendency to focus on one aspect; credit crunches, over-accumulation, under-consumption and so on. These are all aspects of any crisis, the more ruptures in the overlapping dynamics of capital and the society that rests on it, the deeper, more structural and more systemic the crisis. It is the capitalist totality that creates cyclical crisis. The law of value operates via crisis; if too much time has been allocated into one department of the economy, it causes problems in others (inflation for instance). The law of value states that, on average, commodities exchange at their value. If there is a breakdown in the exchange this causes a crisis.

Crises in some branches of production have a ripple effect and drag down others. For instance, after 2008 there was a slump in demand for steel as construction ground to a halt after the housing market crashed because of over-exposure to bad loans by the finance industry. This caused steel plants across the world to be closed, resulting in widespread unemployment.[50] More unemployment is used by the bosses as an excuse to drive down wages for the remaining workers: 'If you don't like it there are ten others who will take your job!' In this way, workers are turned against their unemployed brothers and sisters by rapacious capitalists. Those without work because capital cannot profit from them are labelled 'surplus population', a disgusting term for human beings that reveals the inherent incompatibility of capital with human life. As the left-wing economist Joan Robinson reportedly said: 'The one thing worse than being exploited in capitalism is not being exploited' – the misery and poverty of unemployment is a terrible personal and social blight.[51]

Capitalism has gone into periodic crises throughout its existence, sometimes with devastating consequences. From the 1820s onwards, there were recessions and downturns every year (called 'panics' at the time), until the 1870s, when a longer depression set in. There followed the Great Depression after 1929; the oil crisis, then stagflation, of the 1970s;

hyperinflation in several countries; the banking crisis of 2008. Constant recessions are the scars across the history of capital. Politicians claim to have economic policies that end 'boom and bust' only for the subsequent economic decline to be sharper. Mainstream economists often make out that these 'bad patches' are caused by the wrong economic policies, or somehow the animal spirits of investors and industrialists are low, making them cautious and unwilling to invest. Some claim that consumers drive economic problems by suddenly spending less money. This is a cart-before-the-horse analysis though, under-consumption is only a stage of the business cycle *after* the over-production of capital and the decline in the rate of profits has set in, leading to the driving down of wages, job cutting and so on.

These crises are understood in terms of numbers by economists: is GDP down or up? Are profit rates recovering or declining? Is the stock market in a bullish or a bear mood (confident or not)? But socialists are more interested in the impact on people. These capitalist crises can lead to a 'difficult economic climate for businesses' but they can also devastate human life. Mass unemployment, generational cycles of poverty, crime, urban decay and rural stagnation, mental health collapse and breakdowns, the retreat of culture and public life – the list goes on. These social crises are 'patched up' by charities and religious organisations, who see in them the inevitability of the human condition. We reject that – the inevitability does not arise from human nature but from the cyclical nature of capital and its over-accumulation, that is, the way its success must lead to failure.

An important change in modern capitalism is the shift towards financialisation. To offset declining profits elsewhere, more and more companies turn to financial instruments and products. The Italian socialist Giovanni Arrighi described this as an era of 'financial expansion in which profits come, not from the further expansion of trade and production, but from borrowing, lending and speculating'.[52] Privatisation and neoliberal economics shifted capitalism from the post-war social democratic model of mixed economies, empowering rentiers and the finance sector over more productive forms of capital. Cheap credit for consumers, alongside incredibly complex financial instruments, became the new norm. These developments have changed the dynamics of crises, partly off-setting them, but then also making them even more explosive when they do occur. Today, massive hedge funds stride across the global economy, buying up companies, speculating on cur-rencies and preying on anything that can be asset stripped.

It is worth stating clearly that economic downturns do not end in one 'big final crisis' of capitalism as some predicted.[53] They do lead to a destruction of capital, but this creates oppor-tunities for a new cycle of capital to replace the old, leading to a new round of economic growth. Also, the modern capital-ist state is interventionist and will throw money at companies and banks to offset the worst aspects of a depression, such as Western economies experienced in the 1930s. However, these efforts occur at huge social cost for many people and our societies. We live in a world where humans can literally be declared 'redundant' after a crisis, and schools budgets get cut while banks get bailed out. The socialist argument is that we can begin to democratically plan production and remove competition and over-accumulation in such a way that we no longer have these socially damaging economic crises.

Importantly, the internal economic dynamics within capital accumulation do not lead to an automatically progressive outcome and a better world. They might lead to societal breakdown in the form of climate destruction, but that would be a future of barbarism. Capitalism creates the *conditions* for its overthrow, the massed forces of workers and the socially oppressed, as well as the development of the productive forces to ensure an adequate standard of living for everyone if we were free from capital, but this does not mean that any tendency or economic law will automatically lead to socialism. As Marxist economist Murray Smith argues, 'Capitalism may be "digging its own grave", but it stops short of carrying out its own execution.'[54] It takes active human agency and conscious action to change the world for the better. Without that capitalism is merely digging a grave to bury all of us.

Value and the Metabolic Rift

Everything we are and have ultimately comes from the organic world. Humans are part of nature, but we are a conscious part, in dialogue with itself.[55] Our relationship with nature is not static, we have always modified and sought to change the world around us, to shift or repurpose it, it has always been mediated by our labour.[56] We cannot sit around and never hunt, grow food, or make shelter; we always work on our natural surroundings, changing and utilising things to survive. The metabolism of our organic body transforms food into energy and nutrients; so, as a metaphor, our metabolic relationship with nature is about the social and organic interaction, and its flux and change.

In Marxist political economy, nature creates the *basis* of use values (food, water, shelter, fuel, etc.) and, as such, it is the source of wealth. But it is human labour acting upon it that gives it value, which can be measured and exchanged in the marketplace. How can we judge the price of food or water? They are both in many ways priceless. Is one more valuable than the other? Clearly not (though a thirsty person might *in that moment* value water more than food). It is human labour acting upon these commodities that creates the exchange value for capitalism to measure and price everything. Bread is cheap in most countries because the baking process is industrialised. A bottle of water is comparatively expensive but that is because you are not paying for the water, but rather for the plastic bottle which is the product of a vast production process.[57]

Under capitalism the relentless drive to accumulate and create value as something that can be exchanged to generate surplus value – and thus profit – has disrupted the metabolic relationship between us and the planet in a severely dysfunctional way.[58] This rift was initially caused by the violent imposition of capital, as peasants were forced off the land and had to accept the commodification of their labour power: 'the working-class, or proletariat, and metabolic rift originate from a unique, global process of violent separation of people from their means of subsistence, which also disrupts the biosphere. The ecological crisis is thus a direct consequence of class making.'[59]

What form does the metabolic rift take? One way to imagine it is how nature moves in cycles, 'the water cycle, the rock cycle, the nitrogen cycle, the glacial-interglacial cycle, the carbon cycle' and so on.[60] To this we can add patterns, for instance of migration and weather. The specific rupture that capital brings about causes it to destabilise these cycles and patterns through introducing environmental changes that cause over- or under-accumulation. It started in agriculture, with intensification of farming through the use of fertilisers and pesticides, alongside deforestation, which led to soil erosion and eutrophication (accumulation of algae). Later, with mass commodity production, carbon became over-accumulated in the atmosphere. The consequence is that global warming means that the glacial cycle is under-accumulated

– the ice caps melt. The intensification of farming and meat production speed up the creation of diseases and viruses – such as Covid. Covid also spread around the world so rapidly due to the globalised nature of the economy. The artificial nitrogen cycle is now twice the size of the natural one.

The consequence of this disruption of cycles and patterns due to industrial capitalism is the rupture of planetary boundaries, which represent limits on what the environment can absorb without there being severely adverse consequences. Such ruptures can create dangerous feedback loops which accelerate problems elsewhere within the biosphere. Of the planetary boundaries identified by ecologists in 2009, several are already breached: global warming, ozone depletion, atmospheric aerosol, ocean acidification, nitrogen and phosphorus cycles, freshwater use, land system change, biodiversity and chemical pollution.[61]

It would be wrong to see different ecological processes without humans as peacefully harmonious, however. Nature is red in tooth and claw, and violent destructive earthquakes, tsunamis and volcanic eruptions are as much a part of ecological processes as any equilibriums. There have been five extinction-level events throughout our planet's history – notably, the Permian-Triassic extinction 250 million years ago was also caused by massive carbon emissions, this time from volcanos, which wiped out most life on the planet. Previously they were caused by events within the realm of non-human nature, but the present mass extinction event and global warming crisis threaten the planet with processes and actions deriving entirely from within the human realm. What marks us out is that we are a *conscious* part of nature that is actively destroying the ecological basis for our own existence on the orders of capital.

Another way to think of the metabolic rift is through how capital transforms labour, encloses space and accelerates time. We have described how labour is transformed by capital and turned into an instrument of extraction and environmental exploitation. Capital also creates a division between town and country, destroying nature to build cities, sucking in water, and pumping out pollution. And the hunger for profit and competition accelerates our work and society; the combustion engine, the car, the plane, all designed to move us more quickly. Machines for cutting down trees in seconds, steroids in animals to make them grow faster for meat.[62] Capital is hungry for speed and scale, regardless of sustainability.

The accumulation of capital and its desperate need for a source of power that could be easily exploited and privately controlled led to fossil capitalism. The first factories were powered by water, which was plentiful and sufficient for their needs at the time. But communities can easily lay claim to water, and governments recognise that they must provide it as an essential part of human life.[63] Coal, on the other hand, was more energy productive, and allowed for the formation of new capital through the massive industries required to dig it up. It allowed the capitalists to move production into cities, where workers could be more easily policed and housed without the need for the capitalists to pay for accommodation (as Adam Smith had suggested they should). The need for speed, greater efficiency of production and a greater market share led to the development of new technology, like the combustion engine which came to dominate cities and transport.

The way capitalism has devastated the environment is proof that capital value production is not the most efficient economic system. The only thing it is *efficient* for is producing profit from our labour. Coal is a good example: only one third of the energy from burning coal is used. Burning coal is in fact the most efficient way of producing carbon dioxide.[64] Capital is only efficient if you exclude its externalities, that is, the way that production ignores its environmental or social impacts. CFCs caused the hole in the ozone layer. Chlorine is a major source of environmental hazards. Workers develop a range of health problems like cancer or lung diseases. Then there is the greatest externality of all – greenhouse gas emissions. The best governments can do is to financially penalise companies for outrageous breaches of environmental laws, but they cannot and will not control the externalities resulting from mass value production because that would alter the very basis of the economic system.

As an example, the petro-chemical industry is one of the most profitable industries on the planet, but if they had to factor in the *external* cost of the oil production (the huge environmental damage) then it would become completely unprofitable. After all, if you are one the primary drivers of death cult capital, an economy willing to kill us all for share-holders' profits, the *cost* of that is more than can be quantified. But capitalism has put a price on the potential end of the human species, the oil giants made profits of $219 billion in 2022, doubling their profits from the year before.[65]

Rampant growth and over-accumulation by a system that knows only how to generate exchange values to create profit has led to environmental degradation on a scale unheard of in this geological age. Economic growth does not care about the state of the environment, it externalises its ecological debt and does not even consider it as a factor of production (unless forced to by environmental regulations). This is why there was a crucial shift from Marx and Engels' relatively positive endorsement of the economy dynamism of early capital for its revolution-ary transformation as it created the conditions for modernity, towards an understanding that capitalism is now an utterly reactionary mode of production whose time has well passed. Russian Revolutionary leader Lenin argued that the emergence of imperialism around the turn of the 20th century marked the turning point, when capitalism was no longer progressive in terms of revolutionising production.[66] In a recent book on degrowth communism, Kohei Saito argues: 'The situation today differs decisively compared with that of 1848: capitalism is no longer progressive. It rather destroys the general conditions of production and reproduction and even subjects human and non-human beings to serious existential threat.'[67] The accumulation of capital at some point during the 20th century reached a tipping point, where the productive forces began to destroy more than they created.[68] It is important to say at this point that the metabolic rift is widening and has now become a gulf, one that cannot be closed under capitalism.

The central argument of socialists is not that technological development or scientific advances are wrong. It would be reactionary to call for us all to return to some crude state of nature where we spent most of our time gathering berries and huddling together for warmth in caves. Our future world cannot be one that is shrunk back to subsistence farming, along with a total collapse of culture or living standards. Likewise, we should reject the call from some quarters to dramatically reduce the human population as if we are a plague or virus. Socialists are humanists, we believe in humanity and its huge potential – but living under the dictatorship of capital, with its constant demand to produce exchange value, means that our science, engineering, and technical abilities are subordinated to the needs of a monster. We want to build on human progress and allow for the flourishing of human potential and that is not in contradiction with the needs of the planet – it is only the anarchic profit mechanisms of capitalism that make it so.

Imperialism

Capitalism is a system built from colonialism and imperialism, from a handful of countries getting rich at the expense of others. Colonised countries were ruthlessly plundered, strip mined, deforested and devoured to provide the raw materials for capital growth in the capitalist heartlands. Some countries that developed capitalism first – like Britain, France and the Netherlands – became rich extracting raw materials and resources from others.

As economies developed, the production of capitalist enterprises was increasingly monopolised, with fewer and fewer companies controlling larger market shares. This tendency towards monopoly or oligopoly, engendered by competition, required greater access to more capital to invest in order to outgrow competitors. Companies also grew out of the earlier model of being owned by an individual or a family. Investment by banks or distributing shares on the stock market led to a new model of capitalism. The archetypical capitalist figure – like Charles Dickens' Thomas Gradgrind who owns his own factory – is mostly outdated; socialised capital (today hedge funds, investors, etc.) owns businesses. Finance capital emerged as an incredibly powerful actor. This concentration of capital created the ability to produce greater numbers of commodities than could be sold on the saturated domestic market. The impulse to realise a profit necessitated a search for foreign markets to sell goods. As capital evolved and consolidated, it burst out of national borders and trampled across the world – backed up by each nation's government – creating modern-day imperialism.

Socialists described this era as imperialism – the power of capital spreading to every corner of the world. This dynamic accelerated throughout the 20th century, leading to two devastating wars, as rising powers like Germany fought for control and access to global markets jealously guarded by the French and British. The imperialist powers used their economic might to create weapons of mass destruction; chemical and biological weapons were followed by atomic and hydrogen bombs with the power to destroy the world many times over.

After the Second World War the USA emerged as an almost unrivalled global economic power, only challenged militarily (but not economically) by the USSR. The old colonial system collapsed as people asserted their democratic rights. Even as colonised nations (themselves formed by imperialists drawing lines on maps) freed themselves in anti-colonial uprisings after the Second World War, they were converted into semi-colonies, formally politically independent but bound to the imperialist nations through economic control. The majority of the world's peoples and nations live under the indirect control of powerful nations and their companies.

The imperialist nations lock the poorer countries into unequal trade arrangements; they interfere in their economies, controlling them with debt. There is uneven development. Indeed, when the global South countries are labelled 'developing', this is a profoundly ideological comment; they are underdeveloped by global capitalism, or 'allowed' to develop only in the interests of what the imperialist nations desire (historically speaking roads and railways to transport raw materials). Richer countries relied on net transfers of appropriated surplus production from the global South, equating to $10 trillion a year between 1990 and 2015.[69] This far outstripped any charity or aid that was returned during this time in a patronising act by the wealthy North.

The division of power in the world undermines revolutionary consciousness in the relatively well-organised working-class forces in the imperialist nations. The imperial core countries benefit from controlling international finance, forcing countries to devalue their currencies to strengthen their own, and therefore the living standards of the global North.[70] Likewise, the extensive welfare systems developed in imperialist countries were made possible by the exploitative and extractive control exerted by the richer nations.[71] While these relative benefits for workers in the imperialist nations does not make them totally 'bourgeois', as some have claimed, it does undermine revolutionary class consciousness and lead to illusions regarding the benefits of capitalism – benefits gleaned from the oppressive poverty of people across the global South.[72]

Alongside unevenness, there is combined development: capital roams the world looking for new markets or areas to exploit (either people or natural resources). China is a prime example of this, a country that has seen huge economic development since the 1990s as global capital shifted manufacturing there, creating the world's largest working class and transforming Chinese society. China skipped over many decades of development as Western companies built state-of-the-art assembly lines and factories, creating an incredibly productive economy. The expansion of China helped pull the global capitalist economy out of recession in 2001, and boosted its circulation of exploitation for decades afterwards. There has also been huge economic development in Brazil, India, South Korea and parts of Eastern and Western Africa, as capital looks for opportunities to invest and make money. The Gulf states have built towering skyscrapers and whole cities in the desert using oil money. For some, this makes an improvement in their quality of life, but it is always ultimately in the service of capital and those who directly benefit from it.

We have to be wary of simplistic anti-imperialism that celebrates any country that occasionally opposes the USA and Europe. The emergence of the BRICS (Brazil, Russia, India,

China and South Africa) nations is sometimes heralded as a significant gain for progressive politics, but this obscures the regimes of exploitation, extractivism and accumulation within those nations. China's expansion into Asia, Africa and beyond is not based on socialist solidarity but on calculated designs of capital export and control. Such a view can lead to ignoring concerns about violent state action against indigenous groups or independent trade unions.[73] It replaces the global question of capital and labour with only a North/South geopolitical consideration. The reality is that 'there are oppressors in the South and there are victims in the North'.[74]

Imperialism leads to a central argument for socialism – that as capital has become so complex and monopolised, it has been forced to 'socialise' itself. Capital has evolved, from petty commodity producers to capitalist enterprises, joint stock companies, state capital and global transnational corporations.[75] The most important and successful parts of capital are now huge, and embedded in the economy in such a way that they are considered 'too big to fail'. This is why the capitalist class jealously privatise the profits but, in an economic crisis, require governments to socialise their losses to offset the huge political and social consequences if their businesses start to struggle. Likewise, every major infrastructure project now requires huge amounts of public money, even when private sector companies are doing the construction, simply because the rate of return on investment is often so low (or risks associated with delays so high) that no capitalist would touch infrastructure without huge sums, or underwriting, being provided by government. This points to an economic system which is reaching the limits of what it can achieve based on private property and a market economy.[76]

However, the socialisation of capital is also what makes capital*ism* as a political regime so powerful. We are not talking about a handful of capitalists who own everything, but a much bigger social network of investment, shareholding, stocks and wage differentials that bind people to the system of value production. Even our pension funds make up a massive stake in the profit-making system. It is hard to imagine a world beyond capitalism because it is so embedded in our lives and the functioning of the world.

Institutions have emerged to maintain the power of the more powerful nations: the UN Security Council, the International Monetary Fund (IMF) and World Bank, the World Economic Forum, the G7 and many others. Imperialist rivalries can be lessened through trade, or by creating united economic blocs such as the European Union, but they are not totally dissolved. But capitalism is warlike from head to foot, imperialist nations needed a military that could defend their interests and ensure the continuation of the regime of accumulation and wealth extraction. Small, part-time armies were not enough, powerful military-industrial complexes were required, to ensure the mass production of tanks, planes, ships and, later, drones and nuclear weapons. The US built the most powerful military-industrial complex, with bases around the world and huge cheques from Congress to pay for the latest technology and weaponry. International defence treaties and organisations like NATO (the North Atlantic Treaty Alliance) consolidate the existing powerful regimes, threatening recalcitrant states who do not toe the line. After the collapse of the Soviet Union, the US emerged as the world's only superpower, but its imperial power has declined over time, challenged now by Russia and China as the world heads into a multipolar order that will create the conditions for future devastating inter-imperialist wars.

The militarism of a world divided into competing nation states is a leading contributor to climate change. While politicians ban single-use plastics, in 2017 the US military alone burned through 269,230 barrels of oil a day (the same amount of oil every day as Portugal).[77] The amount of energy spent on producing weapons of devastation is one of the most distorting and damaging economic factors in the world; it exists for no purpose other than to defend the status quo, to defend the death cult of capital accumulation that is destroying the planet.

There is no class peace or sustainable future in a world dominated by capital and its rapacious need for profit. All reforms are vulnerable to being dismantled, every social gain can be called into question. Even the basis of life on Earth is undermined and threatened by an economic system that acts like the Bank in Steinbeck's *The Grapes of Wrath* – it just does what it does. The epoch of imperialism is the introduction of capitalism, with its exploitation and environmental destruction, to every corner of the world. It is a world of terrifying war machines alongside water shortages. The globalisation of capital, caused by the race for resource extraction and the extension of (over-)production of commodities deepened the ecological rift. All this damage was reinforced by international organisations like the UN and World Bank overseeing a world of declining democratic rights and ecological catastrophe. While the World Trade Organisation and IMF have been plunging countries into unpayable debt, forcing privatisations, bringing about the collapse of the public sphere and intensifying extractive economics, all in the name of free trade.

Enough of the problems – how can we dismantle this dystopian nightmare and build something better?

2

A Living Movement for Socialism

One of the main faults with many books about possible post-capitalist societies is that they rarely deal with how to get there. Books on socialist planning are often very commendable as a toolbox of ideas, but they present the new society fully formed and functional from the start, a literal blueprint. But we are talking about a transition away from capitalism.

While the socialist planning ideas in this book can (and indeed must) be fought for under capitalism and translated into slogans and demands to organise around, the overall argument about the totality of post-capitalist planning *cannot* be won through enlightened capitalists 'seeing sense' and suddenly abandoning the entire basis of their economic power and privilege. As such, lobbying politicians or publishing policy papers aimed at governments will not achieve the kind of change needed – as Robert Owen and his contemporaries discovered. The starting point of this book is a revolutionary one, that a post-capitalist society will be built out of mass struggle by many billions of people globally – in fact this is the only way to totally replace the present system.

This chapter will look at why we need a mass movement to build a bridge from present-day struggles to prefigure or establish the basis for a future society. I want to be clear that this isn't a comprehensive guide: if anyone knew the exact road map to socialism, I would be enjoying a 15-hour work week and not spending time writing books like this, so consider this more of a contribution to the debate over strategy. Even if you don't agree with the strategy outlined over the next few pages, it might prompt some more thinking about what needs to be done. However, the vision of socialist planning put forward in this book is based on the forms of struggle that emerge during the struggle against capitalism as it currently exists.

We need a human vision, so any radical change has to be based on people taking power. That means economic democracy alongside radical political change, so we have to talk about workers in the broadest sense as a central agent of that change. While the kind of workers' movement that brought about the revolutionary struggles of the first half of the 20th century might be behind us, we should be careful not to sink simply into social-movementism, as if mass protests will be enough to radically reconfigure the economy. It will be workers acting in their own class interests, united with the social movements, that will create radical change. Revolution takes planning, coordination, organisation and a lot of luck.

The other aspect to this is that we must also be clear that the problem isn't small groups of politicians or professional lobbyists lying to us or 'manipulating the media'. It is the global capitalist class and their rapacious need for profits and accumulation which is at the heart of the metabolic rift with the environment. This means both understanding class *and* the antagonistic struggles between the classes. The class struggle is real, and it happens every day, in small, almost unnoticeable, ways as well as in the form of huge class battles involving millions of people in strikes, demonstrations and revolutions. But class struggle is not just trade unions, it is the billions of acts and events that challenge the logic of neoliberalism and capitalism.

As we saw in the last chapter, capitalism is a system of crisis. These crises can be economic, social or political, or systemic

– that is, a combination of all three. In such periods, suddenly the class contradictions are thrown into sharp relief and the struggle intensifies to a level where the possibility of moving beyond our existing society becomes apparent. In such a moment, socialists fight for forms of dual power, to create institutions based on the resistance to capitalism that can challenge the power of the capitalists' state and potentially vie for power. This is why Marx and Engels were so animated by the creation of the Paris Commune 1871, when the working people of Paris took control of the city for nine weeks and passed a series of radical laws that would have been inconceivable under the French bourgeoisie.[1]

A revolutionary strategy is based on understanding how ruptures can occur in society, how the existing order can go into crisis and what seemed stable and eternal can suddenly appear incredibly fragile and weak. Lenin describes what he thought a revolutionary situation might look like:

> To the Marxist it is indisputable that a revolution is impossible without a revolutionary situation; furthermore, it is not every revolutionary situation that leads to revolution. What, generally speaking, are the symptoms of a revolutionary situation? We shall certainly not be mistaken if we indicate the following three major symptoms: (1) when it is impossible for the ruling classes to maintain their rule without any change; when there is a crisis, in one form or another, among the 'upper classes', a crisis in the policy of the ruling class, leading to a fissure through which the discontent and indignation of the oppressed classes burst forth. For a revolution to take place, it is usually insufficient for 'the lower classes not to want' to live in the old way; it is also necessary that 'the upper classes should be unable' to live in the

old way; (2) when the suffering and want of the oppressed classes have grown more acute than usual; (3) when, as a consequence of the above causes, there is a considerable increase in the activity of the masses, who uncomplainingly allow themselves to be robbed in 'peace time', but, in turbulent times, are drawn both by all the circumstances of the crisis *and by the 'upper classes' themselves* into independent historical action.[2]

This is similar to Marx's description of a time when 'all the contradictions come into play'.[3] As the contradictions that are built into capitalism begin to erupt (and this is not just economic it is also political, social, ecological and so on) 'nothing can emerge at the end of the process which did not appear as a presupposition and precondition at the beginning'. We can call these situations organic crises; they create the conditions for overcoming capitalism, but nothing is automatic.[4] Socialism can only result through conscious mass action.

Resistance to Capitalism Prefigures Socialism

The way our lives are organised by capital forces forms of organisation and resistance which themselves foreshadow (prefigure) a world after capitalism. For instance, throughout history, where there are economic and social crises people have occupied their workplaces and begun to think about how society can be run differently. It is also about self-organisation of the working class in moments of struggle, particularly during pre-revolutionary and revolutionary situations. The Russian October revolution in 1917 was won on the slogans of 'Bread, Peace and Land' – that the working people would get the necessities of life, that Russia would leave the war, and that the peasants would get the land and not have to be subservient to landlords. It was also won on a call for a new kind of society and state, one based on mass assemblies of workers and peasants (and conscripted soldiers) – 'All power to the Soviets'. Likewise, the mass workers' uprising in Italy between 1919 and 1920 created a network of workers' councils which the Italian socialist Antonio Gramsci saw as the embryo for a new kind of revolutionary state – before Mussolini's fascist forces crushed the workers' movement.

Workers taking action as workers has a long history after the Second World War as well. The uprising in France in 1968 saw 9 million workers occupy their factories and shops. The Portuguese revolution of 1974, which was led by rank-and-file soldiers, saw urban workers occupying workplaces, poorer farmers seizing land, and mass nationalisations. The Timex Firestone tyre factories were occupied, and over 8,000 workers occupied the shipyard at Lisnave south of Lisbon. At the start of the Iranian revolution in 1979, workers took over their factories and workplaces and formed *shuras*, committees: 'We have formed and appointed this shura to be in charge of the factory, to sort out the affairs and problems. We have built the shura for the sake of our revolution ...'[5] In 1980 the occupation of the Lenin Shipyards in Gdańsk by the dock workers sparked the beginning of a democratic revolution, one where women workers pushed for the original strike over pay to go even further and broaden into other social issues.[6] During the Argentina uprising of 2001 during the debt crisis, 'worker-recuperated, worker-run enterprises' involved over 10,000 workers in around 200 recuperated firms.[7] Zanon ceramics and Brukman textile factories became internationally famous as they continued production under workers' control after their owner disappeared during the financial meltdown.

Even outside of revolutionary crises in society, we can see how workers' actions point the way to the kind of struggles that can change society. During the French Lip Factory occupation of 1973, workers in a watch factory facing mass redundancies occupied the premises and started to produce the watches themselves, notably with women worker committees leading a workplace struggle against sexism.[8] The occupation of the Upper Clyde Shipbuilders in 1971 caused a crisis for the Conservative government as 13,000 Clydebank workers occupied the shipyard and organised a work-in for six months, finally forcing concessions from the government to subsidise continued ship building. In response to attacks by the Venezuelan capitalist class, workers occupied factories in 2002. The paper factory Venepal and a valve factory Inveval, were nationalised, and Inveval became a workers' cooperative in 2007. Notably, the paper factory ended up employing casual labourers and replicating the capitalist social division of labour, but the valve factory worked through an assembly, electing 'coordinators of production' and paying everyone the same.[9]

The 2008 financial crisis saw a wave of workers' occupations around the world as the capitalist class cut costs to save profits. The Ssangyong car plant in Pyeongtaek in South Korea was occupied for three months in 2009, fighting off a series of police attacks until management agreed to keep half the jobs. A Thomas Cook shop on Grafton Street in Dublin was occupied for five days after staff were all sacked by senior managers. Workers took action at the Prisme packaging plant in Scotland, at a number of at Visteon sites across the UK, as well as against the closures of the Vestas wind turbine plant on the Isle of Wight, Republican Windows and Doors in Chicago in the USA, and Waterford Crystal in Ireland – all in 2009. All of these occupations ended either in defeat or a compromise of some kind, but that is the reality of most workers' struggles when faced with the power of organised capital. What they show us, however, is that capital is not sacred private property – it can be seized by workers, and that collective action is a credible response when faced with unemployment.

One of the most notable workers' occupations was that of Lucas Aerospace, a weapons factory in Birmingham, England. Faced with closure in the late 1970s, the workers formed their own organisation, the combine, organising themselves across several sites and pleading with the government to nationalise the company or subsidise a buyout. The Labour government said no, but the left-wing MP Tony Benn suggested they consider alternative forms of production. The 18,000-strong workforce set up a series of discussions and debates on this idea, with the starting principle that what they designed should be both socially useful and environmentally friendly. The workers developed these ideas into the Lucas Plan, pre-empting the subsequent focus on environmental sustainability by over three decades. This process saw skilled manual workers consider their own just transition towards a better world.[10] However these workers were sold out by their managers, trade union officials and the Labour Party, and their initiative left to gather dust as they were made redundant. Nevertheless, their story is an inspiration for how workers can turn a crisis into a vision of a better world – if only capital wasn't dominant.

Workers at the GKN car plant in Italy faced redundancy after the factory was closed in 2021. They occupied it and organised themselves through an assembly. In 2023, they proposed their own Lucas Plan, to convert the car factory into one that makes solar panels and cargo bikes. They began selling popular shares to supporters to raise capital to start the retooling of their workplace. This is the kind of worker-led green transition which shows the possibilities of shifting economic activity towards a sustainable economy. It also shows the importance of taking action to build traditions and reference points within the struggle – creating a living memory of taking action and building an organisation, or establishing a culture, matters in the development of consciousness. The campaign for socially useful production, not wasteful profit-driven economics, is central to our vision of a better world.

The point is that attempts within capitalism to construct alternatives remain crucial. Cybersyn in Chile in the early 1970s, the Lucas Plan in 1976 and, more recently, Participatory Economics in Brazil and Decidim Barcelona (We Decide Barcelona) are all attempts to introduce economic or political solutions to problems posed by capitalism. Decidim Barcelona was structured as a public-common partnership, the opposite of a private finance initiative, 'financed by public institutions and governed by an open community of public administrators, researchers, activists, and volunteers'.[11] In Brazil, during Lula's first presidency, major cities experimented with participatory budgeting, where local residents could determine how municipalities spent their budgets. However, the key point is that, unless there is political power, then capital will always limit, undermine and eventually roll back (or, in the case of Chile, violently murder) such efforts. Even the famous participatory budgets in Porto Alegre in Brazil eventually became democratic exercises in austerity management when local funding was cut after 2004. Since the people did not control the profitable parts of the economy, they were only permitted to argue over the scraps allocated to the public sector.[12]

We could imagine the following example for instance – a company has a militant workforce, well organised and class conscious. Using the threat of strike action, they demand that any decisions over extractive activities or economic actions without externalities properly considered, must be countersigned by the workers' representatives. This is a form of dual power in a company. The same applies to workers having the right to inspect the books or audit accounts. Another example would be a campaign for a law that allows local communities to vote and decide on whether to allow certain economic activities to occur where they live. Building left class-struggle organisations within trade unions allows workers to take action when union leaders – often ultimately wedded to the maintenance of the existing economic arrangements – will not act. Another form of dual power within our own movement. At some point, the question of who really runs things and how they make decisions must be answered.

Not Just Workers, but a Much Wider Movement

A movement that has any hope of challenging capitalism must be rooted in the activity of workers in their workplaces, but that alone is not enough. To build a post-capitalist society based on participatory democracy will require a culture of broader action and emancipation. Whenever we talk about workers we have to be clear – if the point wasn't clear already – that we do not just refer to white, male factory workers in the West. Our vision of the working class is expansive and universal. Think of the vast majority of women globally in unpaid care work, the so-called informal economy – not waged labourers but workers nonetheless. It is everyone who has no *real* stake in terms of property and investments in the present system. When we talk about a revolutionary struggle, it is one that must by necessity involve also rural peasants, unemployed people, those unable to work under capitalism and people who are initially propelled into political struggle by their social oppression (for instance gender, ethnicity or sexuality). All must have their needs met in a society of scarcity and inequality – they all struggle in their own ways.

It is dangerous to focus strictly on economic issues and act as if such issues automatically become political simply by virtue of provoking resistance to capital in a workplace. To put it crudely, a fight for a four-day week in one workplace is a sectional or narrow trade union question – but a campaign for a law to *impose* the four-day week is a *political* question. There is a difference between a militant trade unionist who fights against their boss and a socialist who generalises the fight against the system itself. The aims of the socialist go beyond the workplace class struggle, towards a political conclusion; the aim is not to endlessly battle an enemy who will always rule over us, to wring only concessions and crumbs from them, but ultimately to overthrow them and their system. For an example, in a strike wave over pay during an inflationary crisis, the strategy is to transform limited sectional disputes over pay by certain trade unions, into a class-wide political struggle that raises wages for everyone. Only in this way, by breaking out of the narrow confines of legal trade disputes and towards a wider class struggle, can the working class prove that it is the universal class that can make the world better for everyone.

This is crucial in the environmental movement. Many governments want to prevent workers from uniting with environmentalists (as in the famous Teamsters and Turtles alliance at the Battle of Seattle in 1999) because they know that generalising and linking up struggles is the real threat. Martin Luther King Jr was shot dead when he was starting to organise the civil rights movement alongside striking workers. Black Panther leader Fred Hampton was assassinated in part for trying to create a Rainbow Alliance, uniting poor people of all ethnicities, the women's movement and others. These were considered credible and escalating threats by the powers that be.

In an age of rampant rentier capitalism and declining living standards (let alone the environmental crisis), constructing alliances of solidarity that can build mass movements and challenge the logic of capital is of strategic importance. One good example is housing struggles, with rents skyrocketing and poorer people especially suffering, a movement that fights for rent controls and expansion of public housing is something that can unite diverse groups. Likewise, workers on strike can unite with service users to form powerful movements, as Alice Martin and Annie Quick argue in *Unions Renewed*, where they champion alliances between trade unions and social movements campaigning around debt.[13]

All struggles, no matter how small or sectional, are important, but a political argument must be won to link up the issues: 'the development of socialist consciousness and ecological awareness is a process in which the decisive factor is people's own collective experience of struggle, moving from local and partial confrontations to the radical change of society'.[14]

A focus on class does not mean ignoring or denigrating the struggles of socially oppressed people that do not initially appear as strictly class-based movements. The fight against racism, sexism, LGBTQphobia and so on is crucial to any emancipatory fight. Socialists must not fall into the trap of ignoring social oppression because it might impact on someone who is not working class. When Taylor Swift or Hillary Clinton complain about sexist treatment it would be wrong to say these concerns are irrelevant because they are rich or powerful, because when they speak about sexism or misogyny countless women will recognise a similar blight in their own lives. Socialists criticise Clinton for being a violent neoliberal imperialist not for her gender.

And it is important to engage with the positive aspects of feminism and black liberation politics. When we think of imagining new ways of living or being together as humans on this planet, these social movements and struggles have a lot to say. This is why the forces of reaction disparage them so much: they hate the idea of the world that people are fighting for.

Ultimately, however, social oppression under capitalism derives from the class formations of society as discussed in the previous chapter. The social division of labour cuts through gender, sexuality, ethnicity or nationality and is a key part of the ideological structuring of society. It justified slavery and domestic servitude, and maintained that the straight nuclear family was the only way to live; it is from these positions that the ideologies of racism, sexism and so on were generalised and propagated. Ultimately, because gender and ethnicity are entwined in hierarchies of power determined by capital and the social division of labour, ending racism and sexism will require an end to the social division of labour, which only ecosocialism can consistently guarantee.

Movements that are built under capitalism often involve people from different classes and any significant social struggle will divide the middle class and the working class. It is important to have broad demands and slogans that can mobilise the greatest number of people, without sacrificing any core principles. A point that socialists often make in various social movements is that class, in the final analysis, determines politics. The Suffragette movement and the civil rights movement are both examples of mass movements where differences over strategy and outcome arose between the poorer working class and the richer middle- and upper-class leaders of these movements. This is particularly important in countries around the world where there are large middle classes/ petty bourgeois sections of society, for instance subsistence farmers and peasants. Marx debates this with the anarchist Mikhail Bakunin, arguing that:

the proletariat must take measures, as a government, through which the peasant finds his position directly improved, which thus wins him for the revolution; measures, however, which facilitate in nucleus the transition from private property in the soil to collective property, so that the peasant comes to it of his own accord.[15]

The central point of this book is that, if we want to save the planet from the capitalist death cult, then we have to think about economic relations: production, transport and energy. As discussed in the last chapter, there is an antagonism between the vast mass of humanity who do the work and those who control how the work is done and how the surplus is used. Economic relations are fundamental. This can be summed up through the issue of ownership – the capitalists own the means of production and therefore they decide what is produced. The entire last period of capitalism, often labelled neoliberalism, wasn't about more market competition as some maintained, in reality it was about ensuring that more of the economy was in the hands of the capitalist class. Who owns and therefore controls the economy is crucial.[16] To address poverty, inequality and all the other blights of our world we have to tackle the ownership question. Class matters because, if we want to replace capitalism with a democratic plan, this requires those who work in the economy to lead on the planning. Inasmuch as manufacturing jobs have moved abroad, this only exposes the internationalist aspect of socialism more clearly.

The State as Organised Violence

All fundamental political questions are decided by force. This is why the police force (hence the name) and a permanent standing army exist under capitalism. Whether it is to break a strike, beat up demonstrators, arrest activists or opposition leaders, intimidate people or use military means to defend the state and the capitalist class, the bodies of paid armed people are there. They are backed up by an apparatus of intelligence gathering, surveillance, courts and prisons to maintain the status quo. Alongside these are also frenzied forces of reaction, who are 'ordinary people' but are inspired to engage in violence against progressive forces. Eco-protesters get beaten up by drivers, right-wing mobs counter-protest against Black Lives Matter or other social movements, men like Anders Breivik or Brenton Tarrant pick up guns and go on murdering sprees.

This is obviously where the question of force arises. The capitalists stay in power through a mix of ideological soft power – the myriad 'common-sense' beliefs that their system is somehow eternal and the best for humanity, reinforced by the media and state religions – and hard power: the policeman's truncheon, the prison system and the use of extra-parliamentary violent fascist gangs if necessary. A revolutionary struggle is one that fights to break up the monopoly of state power and force, and empower the socialist movement to overthrow the old order. Historically that has happened through breaking away sections of the armed forces, by appealing to their class background over their loyalty to the capitalist government, and demoralising and defeating the police and other security services through mass demonstrations and organised self-defence. States usually splinter before they break so anything that ruptures the established power of the state along class lines (strikes by civil servants and so on) is also a good thing.

This has been labelled the 'insurrectionary approach', which is contrasted with the parliamentary approach. At this point we shouldn't get too schematic about the question of what a revolution might look like and there will no doubt be a range of strategies and struggles at play, but we can look to history and see that no ruling class has ever surrendered power totally peacefully. Even in Britain, which had a more 'gradual' shift towards capitalist rule than France in the 1790s, saw a revolutionary struggle in the 1640s and an invasion by a new protestant ruling elite in 1688.

The question of breaking the monopoly on the use of force is also central to building a world without the violence of the police as an institution. Our current society isn't just about a police force that exists to suppress opposition (while also dealing with day-to-day crime in the most limited and reactionary way possible), it is about a world in which we are discouraged from believing we have any agency. People are made to feel disempowered, to rely on this institution which hangs over us and dominates us. The idea of a different way of dealing with crime or maintaining social order is considered ridiculous, even though the modern police force, as we know it, has existed only since the mid-19th century.

It is important to know that there is no 'pure' revolution. Any serious systemic shift in society involving a mass uprising is bound to be complicated, with competing class forces and interests in motion, and struggles for power along different axes of politics. In the fight for power a workers' movement might have to make compromises over aspects of its programme. For instance, when the Russian Revolution overthrew the pro-war government of Alexander Kerensky in October 1917, it was the alliance between the peasants, soldiers and workers, organised through Soviets (councils) that made it happen. To win over the peasantry, the Bolsheviks made concessions to them, which were necessary to secure a united front for the revolution but also were not what the socialists desired for the countryside. Another example could be whether cooperatives will be more prevalent or not in any socialist society – it all depends on the struggle that preceded it.

One of the key factors that prevents a systemic crisis developing into a revolution is the lack of organisation of the masses – so they are not confident enough or they lack any strategy. Workers will often respond to crises with strikes, workplace occupations, mass demonstrations, even riots and violent confrontations with the police, but, in the heat of the struggle, it is too late to generate a political strategy for moving beyond capitalism. This is especially the case when the capitalists reimpose hegemony through compromises or temporary conciliation, which often disorientates people. It takes conscious action, based around an agreed political plan, for any radical systemic change to occur, and this requires experienced political organisers who can inspire and lead.[17]

Demands and Slogans

Once we break out of the capitalist realist mindset, we can organise around demands that open up the possibility of an ecosocialist transformation. This is where new structures of resistance and forms of counter-power can be formed. A key point is to focus on the demands that any movement might raise. As the US radical abolitionist Frederick Douglass said *'Power concedes nothing* without a demand. It never did and it never will.'[18]

Historically, the socialist movement has raised demands that both strengthened the organisational and political level of the working class while undermining the power of capital. Russian revolutionary Leon Trotsky called these 'transitional demands', and they were found in various Marxist writings from the *Communist Manifesto* of 1848, to the *ABC of Communism* in 1919, through to the programme of the Fourth

International in 1938. Any slogan or demand which encourages the self-organisation of the working class, to begin to think of itself as a class that can manage its own affairs and even run society, is a transitional demand pointing towards a different future. Trotsky describes the role of general agitation around slogans and demands that are not limited to immediate reforms: 'Only a general revolutionary upsurge of the proletariat can place the complete expropriation of the bourgeoisie on the order of the day. The task of transitional demands is to prepare the proletariat to solve this problem.'[19] The argument remains the same even decades later: 'In the crises which arise, the transformation of property relations towards or away from communism is the key political question.'[20]

An example of a transitional demand is around wages – for instance that committees of workers should decide wage levels in each industry. Or, in relation to business operations, that workers should audit company accounts every year to:

> explain the debits and credits of society, beginning with individual business undertakings; to determine the actual share of the national income appropriated by individual capitalists and by the exploiters as a whole; to expose the behind-the-scenes deals and swindles of banks and trusts; finally, to reveal to all members of society that unconscionable squandering of human labour which is the result of capitalist anarchy and the naked pursuit of profits.[21]

These are demands that could conceivably be agreed to during a crisis of capitalism – for a time. If the crisis is not resolved by a socialist seizure of power, then the capitalist class will rally, resolving the crisis their own way (which could be through extreme reactionary violence) and dismantle all the gains made in the previous period. Nevertheless, the slogans point to a situation in which the capitalists do not get to exercise complete power over economic decision making. They point to a world of dual power, where we flex our muscles to show how we can be in charge.

Nationalisation, in and of itself, is not necessarily a socialist demand; indeed, the capitalist class is quite happy to national-ise large parts of the economy at certain times if it will ensure the survival of their system overall. So, what would a transi-tional approach be to the calls for nationalisation from a social democratic party? Trotsky argues that:

> The difference between these demands and the muddle-headed reformist slogan of 'nationalisation' lies in the following: (1) we reject indemnification [payment to shareholders]; (2) we warn the masses against demagogues … giving lip service to nationalisation, [who] remain in reality agents of capital; (3) we call upon the masses to rely only upon their own revolutionary strength; (4) we link up the question of expropriation with that of seizure of power by the workers and farmers.[22]

Apart from slogans that move beyond defensive struggles to proposing a better world, we also have to consider the impor-tance of affirming the universal basis of humanity and our existence on this planet. The fight for universal basic services around health, housing and social care is essential to our vision of an ecosocialist future. But what would make these demands transitional – beyond just the challenge to the logic of neoliberalism that they embody – is for these services to be run under democratic control, forging new institutions of participatory democracy that empower and embolden us to run society. Renationalising the railways under state control is redolent of the past, but socialising them so they are free and managed by workers and consumers within the context of a democratically agreed plan for transport is transitional.

Capitalism breeds reactionary ideas; it turns us against each other, fosters hate against marginal groups or anyone who challenges the rule of capital. Socialism is a return of universal concepts of the working class – as a human condition for the great majority, one in which we have more in common than divides us – and maintains that we can build a better world for all. Directing anger at the capitalist class for the society they have created is only the start of class consciousness, ecosocialism comes from a perspective of immense desire for a better world, based on the fullest and freest expression of humanity in a sustainable relationship to the nature and the planet.

Organisation

The key subjective factor in any transition to a new world is revolutionary enthusiasm for the possible. The left often refers to the famous quote from the Italian Marxist Antonio Gramsci about the 'optimism of the will and the pessimism of the intellect', meaning that even if you believe that a particular struggle will fail if the balance of class forces is against you, then you must still engage and fight as if you believe that it could win. The danger of Pollyanna optimism, believing that every one-day strike or medium-sized community protest might be the dawn of a new struggle, can lead to demoralisation and burnout. But the opposite belief, that every action is doomed to defeat and is therefore pointless, is an even worse outlook, as it is a position of embracing defeat before a battle has even been fought.

And all of this points to the necessity of an organisation of revolutionaries who can fight for these politics within the wider movement. It doesn't have to be a party explicitly modelled in every way on the Bolsheviks in 1917, but certainly a revolutionary organisation that can promote socialist ideas and marshal the necessary social forces is indispensable for overthrowing capitalism. Without it, we are limited to mostly defensive struggles and social movements that are not specifically fighting for power. This is why 'changing the world without taking power', which was a popular idea in the early 2000s anti-capitalist movement, was ultimately quite useless.[23] Yes, we can fight for some reforms from below, but capitalism is a political question, it is a system of power and control, of ruthless discipline and violent oppression. It has to be confronted head on and an alternative built that can challenge and defeat it.

It is tempting, of course, to look at the history of the 20th century and conclude that the socialist left 'failed' and 'something new needs to be tried'. But no one has as yet come up with anything as coherent as socialism, and all the new ideas are usually just a rehash of something between liberalism and social democracy, sometimes with a dash of anarchism thrown in. We need to get some sense of historical perspective, which is admittedly hard to do under conditions of modernity (even more so in postmodernity) because everything seems to move so fast and so far and with such intensity. It can seem that everything has already failed in the fight to overthrow capitalism – but we have only been seriously trying for just over 120 years. In the scheme of human history that is the blink of an eye.

Revolutionary organisation which is clear in its principles but flexible in its tactics is urgently needed. Online activism, or only getting involved in social movements as and when they erupt, is not capable of building the kind of forces that can topple the most powerful socio-political-economic system that has ever been created.

3

The Post-capitalist Society

What are the principles of a transitional society moving towards ecosocialism? Basically, the aim is to establish a political system of democracy that is based on decision making by producers and consumers, in order to create a stable economy that is consistent with human needs within a sustainable relationship to other life forms and the environment itself.

So, in theoretical terms, the goal of a socialist society is to restrict and then abolish the law of value, and value production in general, and replace it with a conscious democratic plan of production.[1] This is a more accurate but more complicated way of saying that socialism is an alternative to private ownership of capital and the dominance of the market with a view to abolishing exploitative work. It is a society increasingly based on use values and not exchange values. This involves participatory democracy, workers' management of industry, alongside worker and consumer checking of quality guided by a democratically agreed plan. This is something that must be fought for. Capitalism is not one thing that is then abolished and replaced immediately by something else overnight. It will be a struggle to purge the planet of capitalism, and socialism is only the class struggle of workers and the popular masses escalated to a higher and more intense level.

People say they want to overthrow capitalism, but what does that mean? The key changes that need to happen to move beyond capitalism are the following:

(1) to establish social control over investment and production
(2) to institute a participatory democracy
(3) to abolish the social division of labour[2]
(4) abolition of commodity production.

Let us summarise what these mean before we move onto the rest of the book about specifics of planning.

(1) Establishing social control over production means abolishing the private ownership of industry and commerce. This is where the very term *socialism* comes from. It requires an entire shift in the legal basis of society, away from our current model of private or corporate ownership.

(2) Socialisation on its own isn't socialism. For it to be socialist it will have to involve the *democratisation* of the economy, away from the dictatorship of capital and towards meaningful participation in economic and social decision making. This means politics is no longer the preserve of a minority of politicians but becomes integrated into the mode of economy itself.

(3) Socialism makes our labour genuinely social because it removes the ways in which our labour is stolen from us, through private property and the marketplace. The social division of labour divides us against each other into antagonistic roles and jobs, grants some people a relatively good life while others slave away for a pittance. If social control and participatory democracy are the prerequisites to have any hope of moving towards socialism, the measure of success is the degree to which we abolish the social division of labour and replace it with a balanced economy, based on human needs and with no social hierarchies.

(4) Abolition of commodity production is where we are progressively bringing more commodities and services out
of the wage labour and monetary economy and making
them free at the point of consumption. This is the abolition of the commodity as the basic unit of the economy
and its replacement by goods and services.

Following on from this is the goal of separating necessary work from freedom, to minimise the amount of our lives
that is spent in work and increase the time we have on this
planet where we are free to pursue our interests. This cannot
be done under capitalism in a meaningful way except by the
independently wealthy. Only through rational democratic
planning, removed from the law of value and profit, can we do
this for all of humanity.

The development of modern capital, which interacts in the
form of corporations and multinational businesses is also the
development of advanced planning techniques. Dating back
to the beginning of the 20th century, socialists argued that
the complex capital formations of modern capitalism were
ripe for taking over and being used for social need. Today we
have global companies which organise incredibly complex
supply chains across the world using planning techniques that
could be the basis for socialist planning. We have to emphasise, though, only the *partial* basis, because capitalist planning
is vertical (not horizontal) and does not aspire to integration
across industries, let alone society as a whole.

We will replace abstract labour and the mediation of economics through exchange values with a *direct* relation, based
on 'free and conscious' decision making. As the Iranian
Marxist Kamal Khosravi explains:

free and conscious… are not some moral, utopian, or ideal-istic attributes. These are the inevitable mechanisms of the necessary and sufficient conditions of socialism and its con-stitutive elements. Without freedom this mediator can lead on to another authoritarian regime, and without critical consciousness this mediator can give its place to another ideology.[3]

A study into the role of democratic decision making at Harvard and Yale in 2014 revealed some interesting results. Participants were made to play a game over allocating resources over many generations. When left up to individual decision making, resources were rapidly depleted. But when the researchers added in democratic and binding decision making, the dynamic totally changed – the resources became managed in such a way that they didn't deplete. The collec-tivisation of decision making between equals allowed for rational decisions to be made.[4] All of this simply points to one incontrovertible truth – it is time for ecosocialist demo-cratic planning to guarantee our futures.

Socialism as Class War

As mentioned at the end of Part I, what is important to consider is that everything depends on the class struggle; how it evolves, its contours, its concentration, its moments of rupture and retreat, and so on. What is accomplished in each country depends on how economically and socially developed it was at the point of the revolution. Russia was incredibly underdeveloped but was a very large country that could sustain its own economy (for a while), smaller and less resource-rich countries, with less infrastructure, would have to prioritise basic socialist accumulation of productive forces at the beginning. This *differentiation* means that what follows cannot be a blueprint for all countries at all times, but can act as a general guiding outline for socialist transformation.

Because working-class power is a revolutionary challenge to capitalism, it is not a political project that will be allowed to progress gradually by the remaining capitalists and imperialists. In fact, as long as any countries remain dominated by capital and capitalist politics, then there will be an inevitable antagonism between the two systems that could culminate in war. The capitalist class is ruthless and bloody; they are utterly merciless in their methods and approach. If they are willing to destroy the planet with their own ecocide death cult (which they control!), then what would they be like when faced with a direct challenge to their rule? This is the lesson of the 20th century, ruthless and bloody imperialist violence and sanctions against any progressive regime that dared to challenge the hegemony of the established capitalist powers.

Everything that comes after this point has to be understood in that context. There are several books and pamphlets and manifestos by socialists on what a future society might look like that start from the point at which socialism has already succeeded as a global system, and therefore it is just a question of improving life and rationalising our economy. This is an ideal we strive for, but the reality is that socialism will likely be built while struggling with huge crises.

Since it is incredibly unlikely that a socialist revolution would happen during an economic boom, we can assume that the conditions for a revolutionary challenge to the regime of capital would happen in a period of capitalist crisis. This wouldn't be a normal recession, or even a depression, but an overlapping series of economic, social and political crises. Clearly climate breakdown could be one such crisis, but it would be far more beneficial if the capitalist system was overthrown long before that point.

The lesson of socialism in the 20th century is that socialist countries, surrounded by capitalist states, will inevitably struggle to sustain themselves, just as isolated capitalist states would do if the balance of power was reversed. While socialism can never really be confined to, or function within, any one nation state, it is almost certain that revolutions will likely break out within national borders first. Any credible socialist revolution would seek to expand and include other areas, regions and peoples as rapidly as possible, creating socialist federations as a first step to ultimately abolishing nations altogether. We must beware of state fetishism when we think about the economics of the future.

A society emerging out of capitalism will involve emergency measures; this means carrying out acts that would be considered a scandal by the international community and the liberal legal system that governs the world. For instance, the private property of corporations and rich individuals would be seized, something that would be considered a flagrant breach of sacrosanct property rights. This would land any socialist society in legal trouble in international courts, because the current global legal system is based on capitalist principles not socialist ones. As a result, no doubt there would be economic action taken, embargoes or even blockades (invasions?). There are no easy answers to these problems – the battle to establish socialism will be a difficult one. But it is a necessary one.

Socialist Democracy 101

Socialists reject the liberal notion that the sphere of politics and economics are somehow distinct. Or, to put it another way, any democratic model that ignores the question of economic power directly is pretty useless. Any system of democratic planning starts from the revolutionary shift in consciousness that the wall between the economy and politics must be shattered and that the 'autonomous' independence of the economic sphere is ended. In its place is political decision making at different levels of economic activity that requires a class-conscious and engaged citizenry. It is for this reason that democratic planning cannot be gifted from on high, it has to come from the eruption of the masses into political life from below. We are no longer dealing with merely numbers and spreadsheets calculating the law of value but 'The struggle between living interests, as the fundamental factor of planning, leads us into the domain of politics, which is concentrated economics.'[5]

The initial phase of socialism is the democratisation of the economy. The institutions that people create to start rationally organising the economy will have to be very different to those that existed before, with parliaments and their occasional elections. Also, they cannot be an impenetrable bureaucratic monolith; they must be open community associations with different levels of responsibility. As Aaron Benanev describes, they would 'allow us to reorganise the use of spaces and equipment – and to facilitate the redeployment of labor – in ways that better contributed to human happiness'.[6]

To plan a national economy you must have some form of organisation of government. Likewise, to plan regionally or internationally you also need some form of executive that can make decisions over the economy at the appropriate level. A key characteristic of a capitalist political system is the separation between the legislature, the executive and the economy. Under socialism these distinctions are effectively abolished; the workers' government takes direct control of economic matters as the market is dismantled and replaced by a conscious plan of production. Critics will say that this is a new kind of tyranny, but it is the opposite: it is the first time in human history that our society and economy will really be democratised.

It is not possible to be prescriptive as to what form of revolutionary government will exist after the capitalist class has been removed from power; however, historically, revolutionary crises do tend towards a commune or committee-style organisation of the masses. As we saw in the previous chapter, revolutionary power can emerge from the forums of resistance and dual power from our struggles.

It is important that any democratic forum takes in all areas of socialist society (from the local to the global), has mechanisms for making decisions about provision for the needs and future direction of society because you have to overcome any locally determined advantages or sectional preferences from different groups. Subsidiarity is also an important principle: a central authority should only make decisions or perform functions that cannot be agreed or implemented on a local level. We have to beware of the notion of constant, endless meetings however; democracy also means making a decision and carrying it out, not just talking.

A common proposal in most socialist writing goes something like the following: a national assembly, committed to socialist transformation, meeting regularly, with delegates from each region drawn from workplaces, geographical areas and civil society organisations would form the basis of a revolutionary government. Examples of such assemblies/committees have historically arisen out of struggle; they are not artificial creations after the fact of the seizure of power but are organic and integral to the overthrow of capitalism by mass action from below. The political arrangement will have to be one of democratic and pluralist debate.[7] There must be safeguards against bureaucracy and the fullest democratic accountability to prevent the congealing of powerful cliques.

An important dynamic to consider is the relationship between autonomy in decision making and hierarchy. If there is not a hierarchy of decision making (workplace, local, regional, etc.), then it can take much longer to reach a consensus or an agreement on how to proceed. But too much hierarchy and delegated powers potentially undermines local decision making. This relationship is something that will have to be developed in practice.[8] However, as a principle we can say that subsidiarity – 'What can be dealt with at the lowest level should be' – is an important approach.[9]

One proposal for a democratic workers' state would be for workers and popular councils to hold annual congresses (national or international, depending on the growth of the revolution), which would decide on how to divide up all the national product of the socialist economy. The debates might focus on:

(1) average workload/length of the working week
(2) how to guarantee a satisfactory distribution of resources
(3) which resources are devoted to investments and essential products
(4) which resources are for non-essential products and services
(5) minimum and maximum money incomes
(6) pricing policies for marketable goods and services.[10]

Another approach might be a Representative Assembly, which passes laws alongside a planning commission, which can formulate an economic strategy based on feedback from production units (factories, workplaces, etc.) across society. This would be a plural system with different workers and socialist parties because no doubt in the early stages there would be disagreements over a number of political and economic questions. As well as worker delegates there would be representatives from three other sectors, consumers/users, planners and activists (for instance climate campaigners).[11]

Others have focused on the importance of deliberative democracy for meaningful collective decision making. We cannot simply elect politicians or rely on political parties 'selling' their policies to an atomised electorate. Deliberate democracy avoids the pitfalls of private decision making, because decision making is a public process involving informed debate and discussion, not merely passively receiving 'policies' then putting a vote in a ballot box. Such an approach would focus on the common good, not simply individual self-interests.[12]

It wouldn't be sensible at this stage to be too prescriptive as to how a socialist society would function. In the words of Engels:

the method of distribution essentially depends on how much there is to distribute, and ... this must surely change with the progress of production and social organisation, so that the method of distribution may also change. But [to] everyone who took part in the discussion, 'socialist society' appeared not as something undergoing continuous change and progress but as a stable affair, fixed once [and] for all, which must, therefore, have a method of distribution fixed once for all. All one can reasonably do, however, is 1) to try and discover the method of distribution to be used at the beginning, and 2) to try and find the general tendency of the further development.[13]

Nevertheless getting the political arrangement right is crucial; failure in this area has serious consequences for whether any post-capitalist society can move forward or will eventually collapse back into capitalism.

While there might be different socialist parties advocating different approaches to planning and investment of resources post-capitalism, it is far more important to think about a lively and thriving civil society, one made up of institutions and associations that pursue specific interests or causes, and that such organisations have the resources they need to play an active role in the structures of decision making. Yes, this means that there will still be forms of lobbying and debate, differences and arguments, but we wouldn't be human if we didn't try to motivate and agitate for the things we wanted.[14]

First Steps – An Emergency Plan

On day one, a socialist government has to assert the power of the working class as a social and political force. Crucially, it must also make it clear to the working-class and oppressed people of the world that there is a now a country that is on their side, and will defend and fight alongside them wherever it can. Standing for genuine internationalism, and looking for support across borders, is not just a matter of principle it is also a question of the difference between success or defeat.

Because a socialist overthrow of capitalism will likely only happen in a crisis – it will present an opportunity to present an emergency plan. The scope and scale of this will depend on the nature and depth of the crisis. In a revolutionary situation, any workers' government would pass emergency legislation to begin the process of shifting economic power from capital to social ownership. So first a socialist government would have to enact measures making the lives of the majority much better, with a combination of policies designed to increase their standard of living, increase wages, reduce the working week, introduce rent controls and so on.

The scale of the mobilisation required in order to have any hope of preventing runaway global warming has no parallel in human history. The best examples we could consider are the mobilisation for the Second World War, or a modern version of the War Communism that existed in the early revolutionary state in Russia after 1918.[15] Creating a robust democratic culture and institutions is crucial for establishing the hegemony needed to rapidly shift economic and social activity away from profit making towards ecosocialism. A genuine climate emergency plan, that begins to disentangle the economy from greenhouse gas emissions must also be high on the agenda. Energy consumption accounts for 75 per cent of greenhouse gases so that has to be tackled first.[16] A rapid shift towards renewable energy production and upgrading housing stock, with better insulation, is central to any hope of reducing greenhouse emissions. If regulations on the private sector cannot be complied with (because the capitalists claim they cannot afford it) this will result in socialisation of their assets.

There will be immediate legal equality for everyone within society, irrespective of gender, ethnicity, sexuality and so on, to cover every aspect of life, including pay, work opportunities, clothing and ownership of personal property. The historic injustice committed against indigenous people by colonialism will be rectified through democratic means.

A socialist society would seek to consolidate and expand the social wage as a precursor to more radical de-commodification of all social and economic activity. The social wage encompasses education, healthcare, local amenities (libraries, parks, bin collection), social work and so on. All the essential features of a developed society that are paid for through general taxation and considered a public good would be expanded and fully funded.

Alongside this, the key task is to remove the support mechanisms from the ruling class – abolish the police, sack the generals and freeze the assets of the rich. The principle will no longer be that of the 'rights' of capitalists to own industry and maintain their business interests, but instead the priorities of a society composed of associations of free and equal producers and consumers. A socialist government must also actively repress the minority that are intent on destroying the revolution and returning the capitalists to power.

The emergency laws that would be enacted would relate to immediate emergencies and built on subsequently. For instance, the homeless and the housing crisis would be a priority. The second (and third) homes of the super-rich would be confiscated. Empty homes of the middle classes could be bought cheaply or be required to be rented to local authorities. One key first step to protect any post-revolutionary society would be to safeguard against currency speculation and a collapse in the financial markets that might have an impact on workers. One example would be shifting pension funds from stock market liability towards a safer pension scheme that will not collapse if a hedge fund withdraws its investment. Emergency laws would also be needed to prevent capital flight or asset stripping of companies by the bourgeoisie as they attempt to flee the country. Ultimately though, the rich 'taking their money abroad' is mostly irrelevant as a state bank can just print more money and the crucial material assets such as buildings, plant and equipment can be seized and socialised.

A socialist revolution will seize the money of the wealthy and restructure finance to fund the essentials. A socialist system would also rapidly abolish indirect taxes because they drive up the cost of living, relying instead on a progressive income tax alongside a property tax. This is because, immediately after a socialist revolution, wealth inequality and the capitalist class would still exist, so removing their wealth flows automatically from removing them from the levers of economic and political power.

Abolishing unemployment is a crucial part of a socialist restructuring of the economy. It used to be inscribed as a key principle of the Labour Party in Britain, to support full employment – everyone who could work should have a well-paid job. But that was dropped in the 1970s and quickly forgotten about. In recent years, the existence of structural unemployment has been accepted as inevitable – another ideological victory of the Reagan/Thatcher era. The notion that there is 'no work' for people is ludicrous; there is plenty of work that is generated by society, socialists will just distribute it more fairly across the population. Only capitalism can take the potential of a human being, with all their creative powers, physical strength and endurance, and declare them 'redundant'.

There are several ways to go about this, but the primary way to end unemployment is to end the capitalist–worker relation in the workplace, make the workers the masters of the factories and remove the capitalist owner(s) completely (as a transitional phase they could be demoted to being managers, accountable to the workplace committee). This would leverage the workers into a more powerful position to start to reduce the working week and soak up unemployment. This could be the start of the socialist society taking over their businesses, because there is no real money to be made and so they effectively hand over their capital to the socialised economy.

The fight for the shorter working week is crucial because workers must have time to participate in collective decision making in advance of a socialist society – workers need to have time free to think, consider and act according to their interests and not just come home from work at the end of the day, fit only to eat dinner and fall asleep in front of the TV through exhaustion.[17] The New Economics Foundation in 2010 proposed a 21-hour working week because it would 'help to address a range of urgent, interlinked problems: overwork, unemployment, over-consumption, high carbon emissions, low well-being, entrenched inequalities, and the lack of time to live sustainably, to care for each other, and simply to enjoy life.'[18] It is worth noting that Bernie Sanders called for a 32-hour work week in 2023, while Paul Lafargue argued for a 15-hour work week back in the 1880s, and Bregman argued for something similar in 2018.[19] The reduction in the working week will be driven by both ending useless/parasitic jobs and introducing new technology or production or work techniques. David Graeber's argument about *Bullshit Jobs* is useful here: capitalism is not efficient in terms of creating meaningful work, only in creating work that can produce exchange value, which often means terrible, alienating and routine jobs.[20] The kind of work that a future society will have to focus on as a necessity includes 'the provision of housing, food, clothing, common intermediate and final goods, sanitation, water, electricity, healthcare, education, child and elder care, means of both communication and transportation', to which we can also add investment, in research and design for example.[21] There will also be redistribution of work, according to how difficult or unpleasant it is, or how empowering or routine it is.[22]

To remove the coercive power of the financial markets from our lives, expansive personal debt like mortgages or credit cards would be abolished. Prices controls would be imposed on certain items to make them more affordable. This would be assisted by indirect taxes being abolished and replaced by a progressive income tax alongside a property tax. Then as the socialisation of the economy proceeded a more radical shift would start to occur, public transport becoming free for instance.

These are the initial economic tasks after a revolution. But what about the more complex question of advanced socialism, where the question of abolishing the market and planning production and distribution comes in?

Workplace Democracy

A socialist society will have many forms of democratic control and decision making so when we talk about workers' management, we are not confining political decision making only to workers at the point of production or in the workplace. As we democratise the economy the way that workers organise themselves and their work is central to the new society.

The idea of workers' control is a simple one: that decisions over any enterprise should be made by the workers in that enterprise and not by managers or boards of directors. This is based on the principle that industry does not need the bourgeois to run it, and workers are best placed to make decisions over their work. It begins to undo the antagonism of capitalism – that the producers are separated from the means of production – and starts to unravel the alienation of labour.[23] Clearly this way of working would also have to be integrated into consumer needs, and balancing the output from workers with the needs and wants of consumers is, as we have explained above, a crucial component of socialism. Likewise, balancing the nature of workers' control in a workplace with the democratic decisions of a global, regional and local plan will require creative experimentation under socialism.

The idea of democratic social control over production and distribution which is universal and equitable is crucial to any positive emancipatory vision of socialism. Indeed, it is the central difference of this form of government from any other that has ruled 'in the name of the people' while brutalising them, yet called itself socialist simply because it nationalised industry (in the interests of the ruling elite).[24] Workplace democracy, as part of a wider participatory democracy, is an explosive new dynamic in the economy, not just as a new technical way of organising production but, in the words of Victor Wallis, 'it is also the release of human creative energy on a vast scale. As such, it is inherently revolutionary.'[25]

What is the relationship between workers' control of their own workplace and wider society? As a rule, decisions that affect a group of workers in a particular workplace should be made by those workers democratically themselves. But any decisions that affect wider groups of people will have to be made by more representative democratic forums.

A workplace could decide the following: 'Relationship of workers to their workplace collective: hiring and firing; discipline; promotions, evaluation and training; transfers and leaves; internal information and communication systems; administrative procedures and rules; organisational form; extent and nature of supervision.'[26] Outside of their workplace groups of workers will have the scope to make relatively autonomous decisions over:

> [the] relationship of workers to one another and the physical features of work: quality control; working conditions; methods of remuneration; maintenance of machinery and equipment; work methods, task ordering, job division, job rotation, variety of tasks, and so on; scheduling; what distribution [of] assignments; type and level of interac-

tion among workers; employment of technology (does not seriously impact the physical environment); non-monetary incentives.[27]

Workers' control at the point of production will focus largely on workers deciding their own structures, work operations and so on. A commitment to green transport might focus on a bicycle factory outside of Birmingham – it would receive an order for 2,000 bikes from the local transport committees, who themselves have received information from local residents that they need more bikes to get around. How the 60 workers in the factory divide up their time to fulfil the order is then up to them. They can also say that they are struggling to complete the order, in which case more workers can be drafted in. The transport committee, made up of elected delegates from the local area, would also have a number of workers attached to it who help with administration, issuing bikes, driving buses, and so on. If the local area had a few bike and car manufacturers then they would no doubt send delegates to sit on the transport committee, because that committee would decide how the things they made would be used.

One important aspect of workers' management is to ensure the political and educational level of the workforce is constantly developed and reinforced. Adult education will be free and accessible throughout someone's lifetime in principle, but there is a particular importance for education of workers in industries where they are making democratic decisions. Economic literacy will be essential for genuinely democratic popular decision making because, through mass democratic decision making, socialism abolishes the distinction between conception and execution.[28]

Workers' control is also intimately connected with quality control of products and services. We are not just workers but also consumers, so local committees with access to websites where people can review items would allow for data to be collected on quality issues. Workers' control and democratic participation would also create more opportunities to identify positive changes to work processes, the elimination of waste and adaptation of purpose for a green transition.

Socialisation of the Means of Life

Just as the capitalists turn to forms of (non-democratic) planning during the emergency of war time, so socialists say that increasing degrees of planning and coordination of the economy is crucial for the wars that *we* want to wage: against poverty, against deprivation, against environmental degradation. Monopolies are considered by some to be an evil under capitalism, as they reduce the capacity for genuine competition in any given marketplace, but under socialism they are a useful way of organising and planning the economy. When it comes to the challenges of restructuring the economy to meet human need:

a portion of this problem is already solved by capital in that it substitutes for a number of little independent industries the organisation of production into one great industry in which thousands of labourers are employed. The trusts have already accomplished the organisation of whole branches of industry.[29]

A workers' government needs to decide on the distribution of resources into three areas of economic activity: production, consumption and social provision. The goal is to ensure appropriate allocation while also looking to identify which goods and services can be de-commodified (essentially provided free at the point of consumption). To achieve this, the economic levers of power in the economy need to be gathered into the hands of the workers' state.

This means that a primary task of this initial phase in the construction of a socialist economy is the socialisation of the natural monopolies. Socialisation means anything that isn't private ownership – it could be national control by a workers' state, or municipal control by a regional council, or a workers' cooperative more locally. However the crucial distinction between nationalisation and socialisation needs to be grasped and readily understood. Socialists do not just seize the industries and factories and existing corporate structures and then put workers on the board of executives instead of capitalists. The entire structure of the economy is revolutionised and changed. The old companies operated at the service of capital accumulation and unlimited growth – assumptions that will not exist under socialism.[30]

The key point about socialisation can also be understood this way: as a shift from state property to socially owned property, which 'means property actually controlled by society, and not just by the state as an institution separate from the citizens, nor even simply by one particular group of workers'.[31]

The basis of taking the natural monopolies into the hands of the workers' government is to control the basic productive forces of the economy, transport, fuel, energy and so on. It will form the basis of any plan for economic arrangements. It will also help in hindering sabotage by elements intent on retaining capitalism. The key advance of socialisation of the means of production is that the law of value will no longer determine investment. In fact, the market in capital itself is ended (except on the edges of the economy), and therefore the law of value is no longer the primary regulator of economic decisions. From this point onwards investments are decided democratically by forums of workers-consumers, based on human need not based on profit.[32] It allows society to make rational decisions about the ratio between immediate consumption and investment, between use values for the existing generation and improved quality of life for the future.[33]

Raw materials, transportation and manufacturing are industries ripe for nationalisation; today we would add logistics, big tech and supermarkets. Many of us already treat social media as a collective commons, even though they are huge data-gathering exercises by private companies. They should be the property of a society. We already considered that these companies are largely (vertically) planned and taking over their existing infrastructures would greatly help with supply chains. But we are not simply taking over the ready-made corporations; it is more about a horizontal integration of these organisations under democratic control as part of a wider social plan.

Alongside this the land must be socialised – ending private ownership over swathes of the country. This means seizing the land owned by large agribusinesses and farmers. In the UK it also means taking over the property of the royal family and various aristocrats. This would transform the property relations of capitalist farmers as well as any remaining peasants in less developed countries, creating the conditions for them to work on the land but not be able to individually own it. The public ownership of all land is an incredibly radical and strategic step towards a fundamental change in economic and social relations.[34] To be clear, this does not mean the immediate abolition of ground rent, only that it is transferred to the socialist economy to become part of the social surplus.

The key point is that socialisation or nationalisation isn't an end in itself. We are transferring ownership to the people to ensure that the means of *subsistence* become democratically controlled and distributed. This is about providing a stable society for everyone, and beginning the process of overcoming scarcity and re-establishing a sustainable relationship to our environment.

For this radical shift to occur, a socialist society must violate the sacred principle of private property. Right-wing libertarians and Conservatives are adamant that private property is an essential part of our fundamental rights, but this is ultimately a political argument about defending wealth and privilege; poor people usually have no property, only possessions. Socialists make a distinction between personal possessions and private property – the first is the consumer goods that we live our lives with, the second is the economic instruments of production and distribution. Under socialism, property is socialised but personal possessions remain your own (you will not have to share a toothbrush). However, the a move towards more sharing of some personal items will no doubt occur; lawn mowers is a good example. For nine tenths of the world population that already has no access to capital or property, any claim to defend the right to property is ultimately an elitist argument to defend capitalism.

The key difference between socialist planning and planning under capitalism is that capitalists and their state plan vertically, whereas socialist planning must involve horizontal planning as well. This is the difference between a purely technocratic state, where decisions are made by planners and engineers, and democratic planning in a revolutionary socialist society. Many have criticised the old forms of 'central planning' in the Soviet Union, but under ecosocialist economics, the idea of what is centred becomes much more expansive: this is not about a handful of bureaucrats sitting in the capital city arbitrarily firing off production targets, but a society of overlapping concerns and interests mediated through participatory democracy.

Often, when socialists advocate the nationalisation of private business, critics point to the fact that these companies are totally entwined with finance capital, so how are you going to take them over without paying huge sums in compensation to shareholders and banks? The fact is that, in most cases, no compensation would be paid. We are talking about a revolution here after all; we are not buying out the capitalist class or renegotiating contracts, we are seizing the capitalist economy and socialising it.

But this will no doubt have to happen by degrees. Socialism is unlikely to be one sudden act that entirely abolishes private property in production overnight. Think of it more like a relentless energy striving to realign the economy along the values of social justice and collective control: 'by means of measures, therefore, which appear economically insufficient and untenable, but which, in the course of the movement, outstrip themselves, necessitate further inroads upon the old social order, and are unavoidable as a means of entirely revolutionising the mode of production.'[35] In Karl Kautsky's account, he suggests that a relatively moderate way of achieving the same end:

> The socialisation of capitalist industry will carry with it the socialisation of the greater part of the money capital. When a factory or a piece of landed property is nationalised, its debts will be also nationalised, and private debts will become public debts. In the case of a corporation the stockholders will become holders of government bonds.[36]

Some believe that such an act is impossible because of globalisation and the era of multinational corporations. If a socialist revolution starts in one country first of all, the workers' government can seize the assets of any company that operates within its national borders, including its offices, shops, equipment, any plant or factories that it might have. If the company created socially useful value before, then this will be continued, if not then the socialised property can be converted to do something more useful.

When socialists raise the demand to take over the banks and people reply that it will cost billions of pounds to pay off shareholders and so on, then they are still thinking within the framework of capitalism where private property is sacrosanct. Socialism abolishes the private ownership of industry, including banks. The role of a socially owned and controlled bank would be to facilitate investments for future economic development. The political character of the bank as an agent of the capitalist class is stripped away, but its essential function as an institution would be useful for a socialist economy: 'it would indeed be nothing more than a board which keeps the books and accounts for a society producing in common'.[37]

The abolition of money as a universal commodity-equivalent under socialism would bring into sharp focus the role of the rentier capitalists in finance. Without money exchange there can be no interest charges – this is a decisive shift away from finance capital as a dominant force in the economy. Clearly any remaining class struggles would erupt over such a move as we finally end the power of money as a *thing* over our lives.[38]

Some are cautious about the question of confiscation of capitalism versus compensation because of the way that finance capital has sucked in so many small business owners and workers. Today it is the case that millions of people's pensions, savings and so on are tied up in investments or some kind of capital financial accumulation. It would strengthen the case of counter-revolution if all of their money was simply seized, which is why converting all such shares into government bonds and taxing the wealth from them might be a necessary transitional approach. If so, then any seizure of a private enterprise would likely only see compensation for the small investors and pension funds, not the hedge funds, investment funds, major individual shareholders and so on. One method to socialise companies is for a socialist government to pass a law requiring a super-majority of the board of any company to be made up of workers and representatives from public institutions. This would limit the rights of shareholders to elect pro-business capitalists to run a company, which would obviously affect the share price (it would go down). Shareholders who wanted to sell what was left of their investments could sell in exchange for government bonds.

As to the question of national, regional or local control, that would depend on pragmatic considerations, as it does to a degree already under capitalism. The kind of investment and work that would have to go into building massive solar and wind farms requires nationalisation, but the distribution of electricity locally might be arranged by a municipal route. The key principle is that decisions are taken at the level appropriate to those exclusively affected, the subsidiarity principle. This will inevitably bring about a mix of participatory and representative democracy.

The question of national, regional or local control also points to a constant need to overcome the artificial national borders imposed by capitalism. Rutger Bregman makes a powerful case for open borders even within a capitalist context, showing how, if economic investment can cross borders, then people doing so is likewise beneficial to global development.[39] New economic logics will assert themselves, as the socialist economist Otto Neurath envisioned in the 1920s:

We might for instance reach a stage ... where areas along big navigable rivers would form one administrative unit for building, transport and production, whereas the educational units might depend on language.... The national areas might for instance have different boundaries from those of the health areas. Insofar as sharper geographical frontiers of mores, customs, outlook, legal systems, etc., show themselves, they need not at all be frontiers of sovereignty under armed protection. Only in this way will the wolfish nature of states be eradicated.[40]

Socialism Dealing with Climate Breakdown

Climate breakdown will create huge insecurity and fear under capitalism, as a system of scarcity appears to collapse into ever deeper crises and those few who feel themselves privileged retreat into reactionary violent nationalism to defend what they have. The market cannot provide for people in a crisis, this is why the UN has to create huge refugee camps for people fleeing wars. We know that climate refugees will comprise one of the biggest movements of people since the Second World War, so it is imperative that a socialist society provides accommodation and infrastructure for them, including schools and healthcare. A lot of the surplus of society might have to go towards support for people in dire situations, but a socialist society will willingly take on any responsibility to help people out of active solidarity, not charity. Under socialism we have the best chance of properly distributing our resources, including living space, in an equitable manner. There will not be the usual nationalist, racist voices demanding that the borders be closed to those in need.

Socialism will inevitably have to be a combination of dealing with crisis and also future planning, using what resources we have to build a society of the future for those yet to come that will no longer be in metabolic disequilibrium or a state of rupture. Capitalism has limited forward thinking; the future is routinely sacrificed on the altar of profits today. That pathological death cult thinking will have finally ended.

Socialist planning has one fundamental aim in an age when capital has already started to wreck the biosphere; 'the determination of the remaining resources that can safely be used for economic activity'.[41] The remaining resources need to be ascertained as much as possible on a global level and then a conscious decision around investment strategies for different regions will have to be made.[42] A conscious social plan would allow us to focus on production to decarbonise the economy, retooling factories from making SUVs to solar panels, turning minds from innovation for profit towards social and environmental need.[43]

One of the key advances is that a socialist economy abolishes the concept of externalities, establishing the true cost of all production, services and building (as much as we can measure it) and factoring this into their prices. If an essential material is being mined but causes pollution nearby as a necessary part of the production process then that is factored in. Likewise, if buildings are knocked down and new ones constructed then the carbon cost of that process is measured and itemised. These costs/externalities can either be initially dealt with through a Pigouvian tax, as long as there are still private enterprises,[44] or a mechanism for environmental harm reduction.

An economy that does not rely on profit to make investment decisions can put huge sums into new green technology, such as green hydrogen, scaled geothermal or carbon removal (and possibly nuclear fission).[45] Currently even wide-scale home insulation or mass solar panel production is beyond the scope

of capitalism without huge government subsidies. Socialism will realign these green-tech developments. No longer
will they be actively resisted by capital or considered 'too
expensive', they will be an absolute priority for a sustainable
economy.[46] There is new technology, like Direct Air Capture
plants that transform CO_2 into rocks that can be stored or
some alternative use found for them. Under capitalism these
plants are too expensive and not profitable; under socialism
they will be a priority, to suck the CO_2 out of the atmosphere.

It will be possible to focus on growing alternatives to beef
without obstruction from major food companies and agribusinesses. Land for cows and cow feed makes up 60 per cemt of
global agricultural land to produce the least efficient amount
of meat. A shift away from beef production in a managed
way that prioritised tasty and protein-rich alternatives would
liberate a land mass totalling 28 million km^2, that is, the size
of the United States, Canada and China combined.[47]

The key question facing us as a species is energy. Our
current economy and society is dominated by fossil capitalism.
A socialist energy policy will be rooted in providing a good
quality of life for everyone within the sustainable limits for
the economy. Averages for the energy consumption of cities
and towns, and for individual consumption, will help in determining a democratically agreed level of use that will help to
regulate demand and supply. This gives us a target to work
towards in terms of reducing fossil fuel energy production and
expanding renewables, as well as working to reduce energy
consumption for useless or wasteful activities. Under socialist
economics, regular consumer feedback as part of a social plan
of production would mean that 'lean manufacturing' or 'just-
in-time production' would be a positive thing for workers,
rather than a precarious and stressful experience. Photovol-
taic (PV) solar panels, wind and geothermal will be needed to

provide for energy needs, as well as dams and pumped storage facilities. A national climate service, with a single energy institution that runs the grid and the renewable energy farms, can create headroom (enough capacity even on rainy, not windy days) instead of relying on lithium batteries.[48]

One of the key shifts that must happen is away from oil for transport. Transforming every car into an electric car would also not be sustainable. Everything comes at a cost and the huge amount of lithium that will need to be mined could be very destructive to some environments. Also, it is only a limited resource. A massive expansion of public transport is the bedrock of a more sustainable transport system, which will require the remodelling of major cities built around cars. It will also require a significant increase in rail networks for freight and passengers, which will require continental and intercontinental planning with a commensurate increase in power stations to provide energy.[49] In addition, a massive renovation and retrofitting of insulation and heat pumps in people's homes is already partially under way in some countries, but the cost to the state is often described as 'prohibitive' under capitalism.

Socialist production will also see an end to built-in obsolescence or launching variations of new consumer goods just for profit (the annual iPhone launch for instance). The fundamental philosophy of production will be the Seeger principle; 'If it can't be reduced, reused, repaired, rebuilt, refurbished, refinished, resold, recycled or composted then it should be restricted, redesigned or removed from production.'[50] There will also be a lot more sharing of useful items as communal ownership of things like tools becomes more commonplace. Why does every house with a lawn need its own lawnmower? Such items can be shared out and easily fixed in case they are broken; 'people view whatever they happen to be using at the moment as social objects, as products made by everyone for everyone'.[51] People will still have their own possessions that they need or cherish (like personal hygiene items, favourite books and so on), but there will be a much more advanced spirit of sharing with neighbours. This already happens even under 'selfish individualistic' capitalism; friends swap consumer goods or share Netflix passwords at will (something the companies don't like). We advocate for a shift from ownership towards usership.[52]

We will need serious innovation to solve climate problems. We saw a glimpse into the kind of rapid innovation and progress that can be made with the development of the Covid vaccine in 2020. Scientists working across business and the public sector published open-source reports and collaborated to share data in ways that helped develop the vaccine much more quickly than through the usual methods, shrouded in market secrecy and jealously guarded intellectual property. Paul S. Adler suggests 'we will need not one but multiple programs of the scale of the Manhattan Project' for planning our green transitions.[53]

Small Businesses and Socialism

A socialist society would initially socialise the key industries and means of transport and distribution as a step to moving beyond capitalism. This means that there would still be a large part of the economy that remains in private hands. This is not a contradiction – when any new socio-economic formation emerges it will coexist with elements of the old one for years to come, just as aspects of feudalism existed under and alongside capitalism for years. The key difference is that the old economic laws are no longer the dominant political force. Some elements of capital would still exist but capital*ism* would have ended.

Under the logic of capital, the idea of becoming a 'self-made person' and 'being your own boss' is hugely attractive to some. They put all their money into setting up a business, even though most of them fail within a few years. All this represents is the limited horizons we have within capital, you essentially want to valorise and exploit your own labour and maybe become a petty bourgeois by hiring some workers to exploit as well. Under capitalism, this seems like freedom from the oppressive demands of a boss or a manager, under socialism such a choice seems ridiculous: why would you seek to cut yourself off from the collective aspirations and labour of everyone else?

Small businesses, known as SMEs (small and medium enterprises) would initially still exist and would likely remain privately owned. Workers in these sectors, even under a workers' government, might not have the consciousness to take control of their workplaces. Trades people (plumbers, electricians, etc.) might still like to be self-employed, though they would likely also have to compete with an expanded municipal direct labour organisation.

These enterprises would be factored into the plan through balancing their requirements of and contributions to the socialised parts of the economy. A local fish and chip shop wouldn't be run by a central planning authority, but it would have to buy its fish and potatoes from producers who might be operating under a plan of production. These sections of the economy would also be taxed by any workers' government to help fund the social wage, investment and so on. However, in return they would be protected from the perils of bankruptcy and financial ruin, as well as ensured a price-control guarantee on any consumer items sold.

The issue that would have to be resolved is the way in which the different enterprises are integrated into the plan. Any local area would have delegates from the different work-places meeting alongside consumers to decide on the resources required for local production. Small businesses might be essential parts of the supply chain for larger-scale economic production units for a time. In this way publishing a plan gives remaining private owners a clear idea of how they can invest in their business and adapt their activity accordingly. Iron-ically, the small business owner is taught to fear socialism, but socialism is a better system for removing market uncer-tainty and the threat of your business failing and leaving you in utter poverty.

As a general rule, any small business that grew substan-tially would end up being collectivised by its workforce and amalgamated into a larger economic unit along with similar enterprises as this is simply more efficient.[54] There isn't a lot of efficiency in thousands of tiny self-employed businesses – as they discover under capitalism. Certainly the socialised production units would probably prefer to work directly with larger organisations in terms of distribution or selling (if their particular products haven't been de-commodified yet). Par-asitic middlemen or brokers would be replaced with more democratic collective arrangements such as cooperatives, consumer unions, municipalities or socialised industries.

Internationalism

Importantly, a genuine socialist economic programme is not limited to the national terrain. While many demands might start on the national terrain (for instance, socialised indus-tries), we have to deal with the reality of a global economy. Something as bold as taking over the financial sector requires transnational action and a political movement to achieve it. You can seize bricks and mortar and machinery in a particular place, but so many companies and institutions operate at an international level that this has to be considered as an essential part of a socialist strategy. The era of globalisation and neoliberalism imposes a new, even bolder and more radical internationalism than was necessary previously.[55]

Having a socialist society somewhere in the world that was in genuine solidarity with the struggles of people in every country would be a massive beacon of hope. Internationalism is the watchword for socialism because it ruptures the traditional terrain of capital formation, the nation state. The expansion of a socialist society across different parts of the world will see a profound transformation in relations between peoples. As the dynamics of socialist accumulation and democratic planning or resources spread, the differences between areas that were previously nations begins to dissolve. No longer is there a power dynamic between richer imperialist nations and poorer semi-colonies; instead there is a reconceptualisation of our combined surplus as the collective work of everyone. This allows for an equalisation of resources and the fruits of production. National economies are meaningless when it comes to social planning for human need; as the common endeavour of our shared humanity comes to the fore, class consciousness replaces national prejudices and we are 'brought into practical connection with the material and intellectual production of the whole world'.[56] The key point about an internationalist socialist economic strategy is that it will start to undo the economic terrorism of neoliberalism and the destruction of economic sovereignty through plunder by the imperialist powers.

A socialist society would also play an important role in the global ecological struggle, not just by setting the standard for carbon emission reductions and defending the environment but by opening the road to 'colonial reparations, technology transfers, food sovereignty, land back, the lifting of sanctions, the end of occupations and the atmospheric space [for all nations] to develop freely and independently'.[57] It would act to end ecologically unequal exchange, where rich countries exploit the biodiversity and natural resources of poorer ones in the interest of their companies' obscene profits.[58] A socialist programme also allows us to be more specific about how we conceptualise equity in global economics. It isn't just the geopolitics of the North/South divide, it is about the debt *capital*, as a machinery of profit making, owes to us as a species and the planet as a biosphere, and how we can reorganise society in a way that heals the metabolic rift instituted by capitalism.[59]

Under the guise of development, the World Bank and IMF have held dozens of economies large and small in debt bondage. Despite the promises of debt campaigns, trillions of dollars is still piled up into debt, with countries spending more on servicing their debt than on developing their own public services. A significant issue for many countries will be their debt to organisations like the World Bank or IMF or other countries. A socialist government would default on any debt obligations to richer nations or imperialist institutions, as they would be odious debts based on unequal capitalist relations. All of the neoliberal agreements like NAFTA or GATT (the North American Free Trade Agreement and the General Agreement on Tariffs and Trade), which foster unequal trade with the global South must be abolished.

After centuries of continuous warfare by the rulers of Europe over who would dominate their continent and even the world, after the Second World War the promise of continental peace led to greater integration, resulting in the European Union. But the capitalist classes of Europe remain divided along nationalist lines, unable to properly overcome national borders and divisions. The rich countries still dominate the poorer ones, as Eastern Europe and Greece found out. A socialist society in a continent like Europe would be able to genuinely and properly integrate economic and political relations in a way that shared prosperity.

While the general arguments about post-capitalist economics outlined in this book are applicable generally as a direction of travel away from capitalism, there will be specific tasks in countries that were colonised and suffered underdevelopment by imperialist nations. There are already valuable lessons from revolutions in several countries, focused on mass literacy programmes, education, developing the social wage around healthcare and so on. Often agricultural questions will predominate, as larger parts of the population will likely be subsistence farmers or landless workers. A degree of industrialisation will be necessary to improve living standards and this will have to be balanced with global efforts around limiting carbon emissions. Since transportation of products from industrialised countries to less developed ones is such a major contributor of greenhouse gases, rebalancing the economy with more local industry could help to reduce overall carbon emissions.

From Money to Socialist Accumulation

Dismantling capitalism is not a simple task. Moving beyond private property, markets and money towards a democratic social plan fit for human need requires new economic laws and approaches. Take the most basic question: will there be money under socialism? Some believe that the immediate task is to abolish money, and that doing so is the most direct route to an egalitarian world. This seems to makes sense; after all, billionaires live extravagant lifestyles while millions starve so why not just abolish money and make everyone equal?

Under capitalism money is both a universal commodity-equivalent and an accounting tool (see chapter 1). An indication of the success of a socialist economy is the retreat of money as a necessary factor for purchasing. It becomes less and less a universal commodity-equivalent for all goods and services and, increasingly, is limited only to the function of accounting.[60] But this cannot be done overnight. Even after the 1917 Russian Revolution, the government was cautious about how fast to proceed because the economic conditions were so primitive; 'In order to abolish money, it is necessary to arrange the organisation of the distribution of products for hundreds of millions of people, an affair of many years', as Lenin noted in 1919.[61] However, advances in socialist planning and production will allow more and more items to become free, to become part of the social wage. Production for exchange becomes production for use values. This is a key part of the transition to communism, where the necessities of life are simply provided, and they are valued according to their usefulness.

In the early stages of a socialist transition we would still have prices for goods, what we might call shadow prices, in order to be able to ensure that the labour put into creating value in production and distribution was properly estimated and accounted for. We will still need to understand the value of what is being produced. Retaining some kind of measure of labour is important because there needs to be some quantitative standard to measure the productivity of the wider economy, including calculations or proportions for different social spending and individual consumption.[62] To make meaningful economic and social decisions you need to know the value of inputs and outputs. If we want to make transport free we need to measure how much time and energy goes into transport to subtract that from the total available resources, while also calculating what such a system would add to our society. As such, we have to have a measure of the socially necessary labour time that goes into production – which under capitalism is called value, while under socialism it is the *social product*.

As a rough approximation, if you take the average wage and then multiply it by the number of workers and hours they work, that gives you the available socially necessary labour time. The distribution of that labour time through the economy is the starting point for genuine democratic planning. This also begins the process of separating the 'realm of necessity' from the world of freedom, by reducing unnecessary labour and expanding leisure time for humanity. The key political task of a socialist society is to clearly prove that it can improve living standards and convince any passive sections of the population who have a 'wait and see' approach.

Socialism is the democratic planning out of the law of value as the determining economic regulator and its replacement by socialist accumulation. However, in the early stages of a post-capitalist society, the law of value still performs a useful social function because it gives us a measure of labour time in the form of wages. On this basis, a post-capitalist society can approximate (at least) the allocation of socially necessary labour time to the different branches of production. That is the starting point for changing the proportions in accordance with socially determined goals – the conscious identification of priorities and the allocation of labour power in their pursuit, and not the pursuit of profit. All societies have to measure the proportion of input and output into the economy.

There are still complex issues that need to be resolved. For example, if labour is both social and concrete, then how can you measure its impact properly? Social labour is how you measure planning in general, but concrete (specific, individual) labour is how you measure individual consumption. One option is for a wage fund decided by the democratic forums, where labour certificates can be issued. These can be exchanged for an amount of goods and services that represent the same amount of labour time as the certificate. In this case, the certificate is a purely passive representation of the same amount of socially necessary labour in different forms. The alternative is to institute a form of allocation from the beginning: everyone gets provided a bread basket of food or other goods on a regular basis, and planning for production is worked out backwards, based on need. This would be less ideal as a system but, faced with the environmental crisis caused by capitalism, we cannot rule out some forms of rationing even with the best will in the world. Such decisions will need to be made democratically at the time.

De-commodifying the Economy

As a socialist society advances and reduces waste, rationalises production and mobilises the surplus of society towards the common good, it is possible to transfer an increasing number of goods and services into the 'category of those that can be distributed in accordance with needs'.[63] The expansion of the social wage means that essentials like bread, cooking oils and forms of protein are increasingly made available outside of any money exchange. This is an example of the reorientation of society away from exchange value and towards use values. We reconceptualise what we mean by *efficiencies*; these are no longer about job cuts but about producing in the best way to ensure quality as well as the lowest environmental impact.

In the very early stages of a socialist revolution there will still be commodities that are bought and sold, but the goal is to progressively de-commodify whatever we can. That will be a sign that aspects of production are coming into alignment with sustainability goals, that we can produce what we need without much waste and ensure its distribution. We are beginning to move beyond a society of scarcity. The concept of communal wealth, the social wage and public service are what socialism will seek to provide abundance of. There are limits to abundance of course, mainly defined by the natural limits of the Earth's resources, so we are not talking about abundance as endless plastic toys or fast-fashion clothing.[64] We will have a different concept of abundance and the good life.

If ecological breakdown means that it becomes more difficult to produce essential goods that have been de-commodified previously, then they should not start to be 'priced up' again and turned back into commodities. There will need to be a different system, like rationing of those items. This wouldn't necessarily be a sign that socialism was failing, but that a democratic collective decision had been made to ration products if that meant preventing further environmental damage or because of natural forms of scarcity. If acidification of the oceans continues, then fish might well have to be rationed for example.

How might we begin to pull apart goods and services from prices? Knowing what the basics are for human needs, a socialist economy will allocate products that are essentially part of the social wage. If a worker used to spend $250 on food a month, then that could be directly allocated. You go to the store and you get your allocation of those social products. The aim is to increase this allocation over time, to improve the range of goods and the quality of them. What about items for living that are outside of the immediate allocation? For instance you want to paint your living room a different colour? This is where labour certificates could be used. These represent specific hours of work done which can be exchanged (but they cannot be hoarded as they would be time sensitive) for items that are not considered basics.

Once the workforce has produced the basics that it needs, which are distributed through direct allocation, the remaining surplus is what can be used to improve society. Under capitalism the surplus is always represented by money. This will likely be the case during the initial post-capitalist phase, but, as money becomes redundant as a means of measuring labour time, the surplus available to society will be shown as hours available (how many workers are free to work on a particular project or work stream) and how much product is available. For instance the decision through the democratic forums might be that more homes need to be built using bricks (or maybe a better material will be available?). A million bricks are needed within a month, but the advanced productive techniques allow for around 1.2 million bricks to be made in that time – the extra bricks constitute the literal surplus that exists outside of the plan that can be allocated to other projects.

All of this is about the quantitative measurement of socio-economic activity. Making this more efficient is a hallmark of a society which is utilising its productive capacities well. But the real measure of progress is a qualitative one – the expansion of leisure time.[65] This is the dual shift that happens under socialism, but which capital will always ultimately resist for the great mass of workers.

Socialist Social Reproduction

A better world would not just recalibrate the power relations between labour and capital or commodities and exchange but also the unwaged work that billions of people do every day, which makes up most of the way humans live our lives, maintain ourselves and our relationships, friendships and families.

An understanding of social reproduction and how a socialist system can revolutionise the entire basis of human society is central to making the case for a better kind of work. While it is impossible to say how people will live, the general rule is that social progress will be measured by the move from social arrangements being an imposition or a burden into something that is more freely chosen. No doubt humans will still fall in love and live together with companions, but there will be more housing available for people to live alone, as well, if they so choose.

We must 'understand that the relationship between wage labour and capital is sustained in all sorts of unwaged ways and in all kind of social spaces – not just at work'.[66] The distinction between waged and unwaged work will be eliminated, so as to ensure the full value of traditional 'women's work' can be properly calculated and rewarded.[67]

Women's oppression starts in the family and the social expectations on her to be a mother, to 'sacrifice' her own career or happiness for her children. While people having sex and children will remain in any economic model, socialism removes as much of the burden of the obligation of child care as is wanted or needed. A basic initial socialist policy would be for free 24-hour child care. Under capitalism this is a demand for the state to provide but under socialism the responsibility transfers to the local and regional collective organisations for providing amenities and social care to alleviate the burden of child rearing.

One thing that will increasingly wither away in a post-capitalist society is the nuclear family as the essential bedrock of how humans live. Even under capitalism, modern ways of living have shifted the role of the nuclear family and opened up new horizons for how people want to live. The family will become more voluntary and less imposed; it will mark genuine human love and companionship, not an enforced sense of duty that is disproportionately negative for women and children. Crucially, as general well-being and life opportunities increase, women tend to have fewer children; so this is one of the best guarantors for slowing or even reversing population growth across the world.

But for a truly radical shift in the role of the family and women and children within it there will have to be shifts in architecture and spatial planning. A collective approach to domestic labour will see a huge expansion of 'communal kitchens, housekeeping services, nurseries and kindergartens'.[68] A number of very interesting examples of how 'kitchen-less homes' and other revolutionary concepts have already been developed under capitalism by the efforts of material feminists or socialist designers, but they always come up against the prevailing social relations which you cannot design out of human life.[69] Maternal leave will be replaced with parental leave, which will be factored into collective labour in any given area and allow both parents adequate time with their young children. The choice for either or neither parent to work for a period of time will be down to the family themselves.

There could well be significant work in community housekeeping services where cleaning becomes part of the social good. This would not be the same power relationship or dynamic as modern cleaning services, where better off people hire poorly paid immigrants to do the work that they have the economic privilege of avoiding. Cleaning will be necessary work, both for communal spaces but also in people's homes, that cannot clean themselves. Such work can be done by either men, women or non-binary people and there would be no shame or stigma in doing such work.

Under capitalism, patriarchal relationships and male privilege that the family often reinforces means that many women suffer domestic violence and abuse within relationships. Under socialism, the abolition of the sexual division of labour and the attendant sexist ideologies that cast women into subordinate roles, along with the imposition of rigid gender roles for both men and women, will be replaced by a genuine equality which will see these inequalities disappear over time. With this will come a genuine flourishing of human sexuality and liberation, free of alienation and repression.

Social reproduction in many countries is being thrown into crisis due to the 'age time bomb' of increasing numbers of elderly. Meanwhile, in other countries, most of the population are under 30 but with no work. Capitalism cannot maintain a decent balance of work and life for people. The elderly are seen as a burden. But under socialism people will no longer be considered as 'husks', or simply burdens on society, because all the value has been drained from them. This is also true of disabled people, the constant attacks on their human needs (mobility equipment, specially designed housing, social welfare) will end because we will have ended the reactionary view of people's worth as being linked only to whether they are in 'hard-working families'.

Under capitalism, pensions are often a fraught subject. Often they are invested in complex financial instruments that are then interwoven into the stock market and subject to feckless and corrupt capitalists pillaging funds for their own personal gain. A pension is only deferred wages after all, and the fact that so many workers go without, or have to boost their meagre end-of-life money by owning houses as property or investing in shares (or working until you die) is a testimony to the failure of capitalism to undertake due care for those who no longer work. Under the initial stages of socialism pensioners will be fully cared for, the cost of their care borne out of the general social wage.[70]

Will There be Restaurants under Socialism?

There was a rigorous and lively debate on social media in 2022 over whether there would be restaurants under socialism.[71] Some took the position that there would not be because restaurants are by their very nature about status, and staff bringing you food, which appears servile. They based this argument on the reality of some restaurants under capitalism, but how would it be any better under socialism? Also, if socialism is the culmination of our rights as individuals, then how does that square with having to leave your home to eat in a canteen?

It is useful to think about the fight under capitalism for communal kitchens and eating spaces. This includes the feeding of children in schools, workplace canteens and leisure facilities that allow for food in the evening. Between 1940 and 1947, there were 2,000 National Restaurants in Britain, which offered cheap food for people to help provide sustenance during war-time rationing.[72] During the First World War, there were National Kitchens operated by local authorities which were proper restaurants with low prices.[73] In Germany the Social Democrat Party promoted the ideas of Lily Braun, who advocated a movement called '*Einküchenhaus*', the single-kitchen communal building, a step towards freeing working women from domestic cooking and cleaning.[74] The Soviet Union had communal living units called *kommunalka*, where multiple families shared kitchens and other facilities, though their design meant that lack of privacy was a concern for some people.

In a socialist society, communal eating places will still exist, though in a very different way. In the initial stages of socialism, restaurants will likely still be privately owned but will have to pay higher wages and reduce the working time of their staff in accordance with the new socialist economics. Waiting staff will no longer rely on tips to survive. In that sense it is only another example of how small businesses will operate under early socialism. There will likely be different types of eating out, from the canteen to the more salubrious restaurants, depending on taste and requirements. People will still enjoy going out to eat, either because they don't want to cook at home or they are taking time to go out with friends or sexual partners.

One aspect of socialism will be to share essential aspects of life as much as possible to reduce waste and ensure efficiencies for services. Food is one of them – lots of communities will no doubt collectivise cooking and cleaning, both to reduce domestic chores and because it is cheaper. From an ecological point of view, a lot of food is wasted in each household so a better distribution of food in a cooperative space will make more sense.

Communal cooking, kitchens and laundry facilities in urban areas are a crucial part of the fight for democratic control over social reproduction and freeing women from domestic chores. We cannot rely simply on an ideological shift to free women from domestic servitude, society has to create the material conditions to undermine the historic role of women as domestic labourers. In the context of the environmental question, communal living will likely become a more popular and also rational way of living. This doesn't mean all living in a big house together (though for some people that is desirable), but more of the chores and work associated with social reproduction will be shared out.[75]

But we should also extend this. There will be a plethora of theatres, clubs, meeting halls, art galleries, drinking establishments and all kind of other spaces run under the communal control of the local community. You don't need a rigid plan for entertainment, dictated by local government, but something far more enriching and collaborative that meets the needs of people.[76]

Trade with Capitalist Countries

While any socialist movement must seek to internationalise the revolution wherever possible, even in capitalist countries the role of trade and diplomatic relations is important. One of the key tasks for any socialist economy is to ensure social and environmental justice. Trade deals could be prioritised for countries with better workers' conditions, trade union rights can be written into trade deals, free movement for people can be included in any trade deals signed between countries.

This can be organised through a state monopoly on foreign trade. A socialist society will need to trade with other countries which will still be capitalist, but the danger is that separate enterprises trade bilaterally. This means they inevitably compete with the commodities that are still manufactured and priced according to the law of value. This competition potentially undermines the conditions in the socialist economy, forcing a race to the bottom.

Writing about the early Soviet economy, Trotsky and Lenin defended the principle of the state monopoly on foreign trade. Lenin referred to 'the unquestionable need to maintain and consolidate the foreign trade monopoly … there can be no concessions on this matter'.[77] Trotsky added that what really mattered was the development of the productive forces to ensure that Russian products were as good as anything that could be purchased abroad:

> The monopoly of foreign trade is a powerful factor in the service of socialist accumulation – powerful but not all-powerful. The monopoly of foreign trade can only moderate and regulate the external pressure of the law of value to the extent that the value of Soviet products, from year to year, comes closer to the value of the products on the world market.[78]

This was the view of Lenin when he argued that, as Soviet Russia 'will be totally unable to build up its own industry and make Russia an industrial country unless it has the protection, not of tariffs, but of the monopoly of foreign trade'.[79] Tariffs only hurt the workers of other countries, potentially driving foreign businesses to bankruptcy through state-imposed artificial barriers to trade.

How would the state monopoly work? If you are trading computers and the computers made in a socialist country are more expensive, for instance because of higher wages, then the state planning department can regulate the prices to make the goods still competitive on the world market. For instance, an Equalisation Fund could match the difference between the prices set by the workers government and global prices.

Foreign trade also allows for an expansion of socialist values abroad, for instance preferencing trade with countries that supported workers' rights and independent trade unions, and that upheld environmental regulation.

Control over foreign trade has historically been important in largely agricultural economies because it ensures food security and allows for price support on agricultural imports.

For trade, any democratic plan must ensure the distribution of goods. This means not only socialisation of transport but also of warehouses and depots. Proper audits of all goods coming into any one warehouse are essential to ensure accurate records.

For a long time, petty trade by small capitalist enterprises or individuals will no doubt continue. The primary task of any socialist government is to ensure those goods produced by the socialised parts of the economy are properly allocated. While laws preventing price gouging by capitalists in times of crisis will be essential, ultimately the initial phase of socialism will see a struggle between socialist and capitalist elements within the economy and the best way to ensure the non-capitalist sector wins is to produce better quality goods more cheaply. Ultimately, however, a socialised and democratically planned part of the economy is incompatible with an economy where the law of value and marketplaces are determinant as economic regulators: one must triumph over the other (see the section on market socialism, in chapter 5).

Incentives and Needs

Revolutionary socialism represents a fundamental break in our previous experience of labour as something that is forced upon us, something that we are compelled to do through fear of starvation. Thinking of a different world, German Marxist August Bebel explained that:

> labour organised on the basis of complete freedom and democratic equality, where it is each for all and all for each, hence, where full solidarity reigns, will generate a desire to create and a spirit of emulation not to be found anywhere in

the economic system of today. This creative impulse affects the productivity of labour as well.[80]

John Stuart Mill also argued for a kind of socialist emulation to replace outright individualistic competition; 'A rivalry as to who can best serve the common welfare, is a sort of competition that Socialists do not repudiate.'[81]

In a post-capitalist society, what mechanism will replace the profit motive as the guiding principle of economic organisation? In the early stage of socialism, when the profit motive is being systematically reduced and removed, prices will much more accurately reflect the cost of production. This means that falling prices will drive efficiency and productivity in a direct way, not mediated through the needs of profit and the nexus of market relations. This will be the 'reward for the common effort' which can inspire us to improve the quality of our work, otherwise mistakes, errors, botched production and badly provided services will only increase labour time as others have to fix the problem. This means no falling prices.

This is why higher wages for some workers 'doing a better job' isn't the way forward. True, it might be used in specific situations, but as a solution to the question of incentives it is too limited, too bourgeois. Higher wages will just mean some people have a glut of money. It would just replicate wealth imbalances that we are trying to abolish. If there is a surplus being produced, then it is no good it sitting in people's bank accounts. It would potentially lead to claim and counterclaim between workers at different stages of the production process: some workers make a tool that makes farming much easier, but it hasn't made the lives of those toolmakers easier, so how should they benefit?

The first and most important incentive is to reduce the working time needed to produce anything. If you can introduce new technology or working techniques that can do the work of the same quality more quickly then they would be introduced, lifting the burden from workers. This would reduce prices and free up more leisure time. This is the true mark of a society that is becoming both more equal and more efficient. Marx even describes the 'economy of time' as 'the first economic law on the basis of communal production'.[82] A better, more rational way of organising our labour time as a species will create the conditions for more relaxation, time for hobbies and interests and to be with friends, lovers, extended family and so on.

The second incentive is that if less energy and labour is being put into any product, then the overall cost of production drops. Farm tools designed by engineers, manufactured and then distributed to farmers will increase productivity and make food cheaper, which benefits every worker along the supply chain. This is why falling *prices* are the benchmark of progress because then everyone benefits. We can already see, even under capitalism, how improvements in agriculture and farming drove down food prices for many decades before the inflationary shifts of 2022 exploded.

However, a truly revolutionary new society will require a conscious shift away from current modes of thinking about what makes us happy. A socialist society is driven by humans who have different priorities and these must be understood in relation to a higher ideal – that equilibrium with the planet and wider community is a good thing. There is no doubt the current world of rampant consumerism will be consigned to the past if such a shift is made. As materialists, socialists know that ideas come from our material world around us, that we are products of our environment, but also that we can change and shift our environment.[83]

Pat Devine says that the shift from the capitalist mindset to a socialist one is between 'compensatory consciousness' and 'emancipatory consciousness'. Compensatory consciousness is about desiring consumer goods to feel better about your life of alienated labour and oppression. Emancipatory consciousness is about collective and collaborative work for the social good, which of course includes your own personal good.

Some will argue that any restriction on untrammelled consumerism will be met with a harsh reaction, as humans always cling to their possessions, their desperate need for 'stuff'. Ecosocialists have a more optimistic view of humanity, as Michael Löwy explains:

> ecosocialism is based on a reasonable expectation, which was already held by Marx: the predominance, in a society without classes and liberated of capitalist alienation, of 'being' over 'having', i.e. of free time for the personal accomplishment by cultural, sportive, playful, scientific, erotic, artistic and political activities, rather than the desire for an infinite possession of products.[84]

This will also affect our view of labour. The transition was described by William Morris as a move away from an 'incentive to labour to replace the fear of starvation, which is at present our only one. [Under socialism,] the true incentive to happy and useful labour must be pleasure in the work itself.'[85] This is a political shift from labour which is imposed on us to work which is a collective experience based on entirely different values.

A crucial point to make is that the idea of human wants and needs changes over time. There is no static human ideal for what a human wants (beyond the basics of sustenance and shelter, but even then humans want different kinds of sustenance, are happy with different types of shelter, depending on the climate, for instance, whether it is cold or tropical) and, as such, a different society will inevitably see some desires that were popular under capitalism and class-based society wither away and be replaced by new urges and interests.

From Individual to Social

Moving from individual wealth and resources to the social resources of society being deployed for collective need is the marker of general progress. As different class societies have emerged via revolutions throughout history, they have all seen different social forces fighting over the surplus. But most shifts in class societies have been moves between one elitist class hierarchy and another. A socialist revolution is the first organised attempt to revolutionise society away from control by a tiny minority towards the majority. This inevitably also requires a move towards redistribution of wealth and power. On an essentially human level, it means an understanding of freedom that is genuinely revolutionary: 'Freedom is not realised in the individual set against a dominating society. Socialist freedom would be a continuous, self-reproducing process of empowering individuals to contribute to social formation in ways that best realise their own need-satisfying powers.'[86]

Reactionaries baulk in horror at the idea of 'collectivism' or anything that seems to undermine the supremacy of the individual and prioritise their rights. Socialism is not a destruction of the individual but the realignment of our individual and collective needs, where the rights and needs of the individual are understood within the wider collective. Marx talks about the social individual, explicitly criticising the idea that economics is simply about Robinson Crusoe types, individuals with no connection to other humans.[87]

There are some today on the libertarian wing of politics, particularly popular in the hyper-bourgeois political and economic culture of the US, who deride all talk of collectivism as a tyranny against the individual. Marxists do not start from individuals but from class struggle. Socialist political economy asks: what can the working class do as the most productive humans on the planet to resolve any particular issue for the benefit of humanity? We know that the power of the working class comes from their collective strength in their workplace, in their communities, on mass demonstrations.

The problem with the idea of 'pure freedom' under capitalism essentially equating to freedom from any form of government is that it is utterly unrealistic in any complex society where there has to be public sector provision for education, health, roads, social care and so on. Its proponents take their view of capitalism from the early 19th century, adopting a pioneer spirit of ultimate bourgeois freedom, without much government to interfere in business and therefore money.

On a more philosophical level, this is a view of freedom totally linked to capitalism but assuming some ahistorical truth. Unrestrained capitalism also places severe limits on human life and happiness because someone getting rich always ultimately requires other people's labour. This is the reality of our conditioning under capitalism, to focus on exclusion and scarcity always as a war of all against all and a zero sum game in which some get rich at others' expense.

Those who exalt the individual over any attempt to socialise the economy under democratic control merely champion the ungoverned and alienating laws of the market to decide our fates. They claim that their individual rights trump anything else, but when this is examined it is merely their right to exploit, to enrich themselves, no matter the cost. They adore the hidden hand of the market, representing the inhuman logic of capital, and hate the idea of a popular control. Socialists propose a different path. Those who defend the 'free market' are in fact only defending the power of the invisible leviathan of the law of value to control and determine their lives.[88] This is understandable if you are a capitalist; it is ridiculous if you are a worker or poor.

As socialist economist Ernest Mandel makes this argument around the importance of proper resource distribution to meet human need: 'When famine devastates the Sahel, is there anyone who would condemn food distribution … [of] physical rations to the starving as a "dictatorial" allocation reducing them to "serfs" – where selling food to them would make them "freer"?'[89]

There is a common held criticism of socialism that it is about the destruction of the individual's ability to express themselves.[90] The usual complaint is that everyone under socialism will have to dress the same and eat the same foods. Of course this ironically misses just how homogenised capitalism has become and the degree of routine we have in our lives caused by monopoly capitalism – every high street in the West looks very similar. Eliminating poverty and a culture based on manufactured wants from advertising will allow for a true flourishing of the human as an individual: 'The goal of socialism is not so much the socialisation of the person as the personalisation of society – that is, the fullest possible development of the unique personality of *each* individual.'[91]

Socialism will not create uniform humans who all think and act the same, it is capitalism that encourages conformity and subordination of our individuality to the *diktats* of the market. Our variety of personalities (maybe more personalities than even Charles Fourier imagined!) and manifold

desires is one of the amazing hallmarks of our species. Socialism will only abolish the way that different abilities between
people become institutionalised as different socio-economic
statuses (also we do not know the full extent to which differences in status affect abilities, private schooling, parents
networked into the corporate world, etc.) Our differences will
complement each other; if you are very good at singing but
I am better at playing an instrument then that is potentially
complementary. Likewise, perhaps I am better with dealing
with people's emotional problems and you are better at organising events. Neither of these skills will be considered better or
worth more than the other.[92]

Looking at the problems of humanity through a social or
collective lens has a number of obvious benefits, from democratic inclusion of the majority in deciding their own fate
to the economies of scale that come from a national health
service or modern farming techniques.

The socialisation of humanity is of course not a new thing
– we have always been social beings. But it will allow proper
social relations between us that are no longer mediated by the
marketplace. We will be released from reified or fetishised
thoughts about the world. Our humanity will no longer be
emaciated or mutilated by the market, our economy becomes
a society as what was previously stripped down to 'economic
activity' is now social activity in which we exist in an open and
clear relationship to each other, and what we are making and
doing as a species.

The transition towards a conscious plan of socialist democracy clearly has implications in terms of the position of people
who might otherwise have been considered 'geniuses', inven-
tors, designers, entrepreneurs and so on. Capitalism exalts such
individuals and argues there would be no space for them under
socialism. This is very far from the truth. Socialism as a col-

lective endeavour in which individual brilliance isn't hoarded or only exploited for personal gain, where such brilliance can flourish and benefit all of humanity much more equitably, in this way provides a better reward for talent than capitalism. Capitalist society only benefits a small number of such gifted and talented individuals, most will never realise their full capabilities. As the radical biologist Stephen Jay Gould said; 'I am, somehow, less interested in the weight and convolutions of Einstein's brain than in the near certainty that people of equal talent have lived and died in cotton fields and sweatshops.'[93]

A Society that Can Make Mistakes ... and Learn

Socialism is not a perfect model of human society. Such a thing is impossible as long as there is potential scarcity, and conflicting views and debates over economic and political decisions. However, it will be a *superior* society to what we have now. One of the problems under capitalism is that catastrophic decisions can be made by captains of industry, middle managers, or bankers and financiers that have a huge impact on wider society. Market forces might punish them (Enron and Lehman Brothers went out of business, for instance) but there is no democratic way to hold them to account or correct their mistakes.

Likewise, although democratic planning is a far better way to manage our economic affairs than market-based capitalism, we have to be clear that it is not in itself a magic solution to every problem: 'Planning is not equivalent to "perfect" allocation of resources, nor "scientific" allocation, nor even "more humane" allocation. It simply means "direct" allocation ...'[94] To put it another way, democratic planning will not totally overcome all the 'messiness' of human economic activity.[95] As socialism is about the democratisation of the economy and the active participation of humans in decision making at every level, it will have to be a society that recognises human plurality and the possibility of human error. The crucial shift is to create the material conditions to learn and improve, to evolve our methods and practices collectively. The Paris Commune did not claim to be infallible, in fact it published clear reports on its discussions and agreements precisely to inform the public of what was being done to allow for democratic debate on its shortcomings.[96]

Any system of workers' democracy will lead to mistakes being made, and there is no revolutionary socialist party in the world that doesn't make political mistakes. But under socialism there will be repercussions that will have to be dealt with and learned from. The Soviet economist Leontief was clear about planning: 'A plan is not a forecast. The whole idea of planning assumes the possibility of choice among alternative feasible scenarios.'[97] What kind of alternative feasible scenarios might there be? Devine points to some examples in earlier stages of socialism; a production unit closing, inflation, or local resources being over-consumed if proper care isn't taken in terms of planning.[98] Some might query if that means that socialism is capable of giving rise to the same problems as capitalism, to which the answer is 'not the same, but similar'. The key difference is that democratic involvement of workers and consumers, planners and activists, will allow society to learn and make better decisions going forward, rather than relying on the market to correct problems.[99]

The socialist historian John Riddell also defends a plural approach:

A workers' and farmers' government will seek to test conflicting conceptions by permitting different organs of government and economic management to implement divergent conceptions and varying priorities. Such a diversity must be restricted, of course, since resources are limited and the interests of working people in their totality must be defended. Nonetheless, a society on the road to socialism, both in its debates and its economic practice, will be characterised by a diversity of approach.[100]

A socialist system will have to address a range of isuses, particularly in the context of global warming. Aaron Benanev gives some examples: 'How to produce energy, how much meat to eat, how to make reparations for the legacies of colonialism, how to organise climate migration, and what kinds of geo-engineering to engage in, if any, are contentious issues that offer different futures to humankind.'[101] Decision making will happen at different levels, with different degrees of expertise. Some decisions will require technical or procedural knowledge where different proposals are put out for a final decision.[102] The lesson of previous models (like Yugoslavia) is to ensure that a layer of experts doesn't become the *de facto* decision makers because everyone else feels too ignorant or unknowledgeable to engage.

New Technology

The introduction of new technology and more advanced labour systems under socialism will result in the reduction of working time and the cheapening of products and services. Workers will not be disadvantaged by new technology because it will be at the service of society and not capital.

New technology will also help reduce boring and repetitive work which is psychologically unproductive. This can be the most alienating form of labour as you finish your work feeling stressed, almost zombie-like. A key task of a workers' society is to reduce the amount of time spent on this kind of work to a minimum and to share work that cannot be automated out.

This means a radical reconceptualisation of the social use of technology; 'The enhancement of use values and the corresponding restructuring of needs now becomes the social regulator of technology rather than, as under capital, the conversion of time into surplus value and money.'[103] The nature of a post-capitalist society will have to be completely political, in part because the distinction between economics and politics is over, and because the future of humanity faces some tough decisions which will require serious strategic decision making. This is also why socialist political economy cannot be reduced to an algorithm or advanced computing; humans will need to make the important decisions. If they get it wrong, there must be ways to correct mistakes and overcome contradictions within the social planning and decision-making process.

And technology will be used to assist in socialist democratic decision making. In a powerful argument for the formation of a techno-scientific Planning Daemon to help process information and assist in decision making, Max Grunberg outlines the key processes that must occur in a socialist society. Any decision must:

> begin *ex ante* with forecasts to determine future demand; the second step consists in a planning process to discover the optimal means to best fulfil this target; third, production itself takes place; and fourth, finally the executed plan is subject to a validation process *ex post* in consumption, which will alter future demand expectations.[104]

Artificial Intelligence backed systems can help process vast amounts of data and provide accurate predictions for consumer trends – they are already in use by capitalist corporations like Amazon. But such a system will always ultimately be subordinated to human decision making on investments and strategic goals such as which energy supply to use.

Such technology will vastly improve human society and allow us more free time, but it will also require a greater degree of technological literacy around coding and mathematics to manage the data and improve it in a democratic way, alongside 'robust civic institutions'. Technology must be subordinated to human need and desire, rather than something that dictates and determines it.

We All Become Wealthy

> For capitalism is already essentially abolished once we assume that it is enjoyment that is the driving principle and not enrichment itself.
>
> Marx[105]

If GDP growth doesn't make people happy then what does? If we free ourselves from the way that capital constrains and determines our worldview, how everything is commodified and sold to us, then we can begin to trace the outline of a future world with a different set of priorities.

It is wrong to see human needs as static; our conception of what we want and need will evolve and change over time because it is historically constituted. We are social beings and our social needs both created society and are themselves created by society. It wasn't a human need to have the internet in the 1980s, but now it is an essential part of human life.[106] Socialism is also not based on a utopian idea of everyone suddenly becoming 'new humans' who suppress their existing wants and needs under capitalism. It is about a better world, a more humane world, that is built out of the existing struggles of daily life.

It is already widely recognised that massive expansions of universal public services are far more important to people's daily lives than the abstraction of economic growth. Having free health care, free transport, free education and free leisure facilities, alongside well-maintained parks and commons, is far more beneficial for people and wider society than *only* increasing wages.[107]

Of course pro-capitalists reply that 'nothing is free', meaning that everything is paid for through taxation or some other fiscal means if it can be accessed for free. This is why introduction, under capitalism, of a progressive tax on big business and wealth is so important to fund these universal public services. Under socialism, the de-commodification of key parts of society will take the place of taxation, as more and more public goods are made available through the general surplus in society.

The universal nature of public services is crucial too. Socialists oppose means testing because we oppose a two-tier system (a better, paid-for one for the rich, and a cheaper, worse quality one that lower-income people can access for free) and also because the process of proving you are poor is humiliating. Everyone gets the same excellent quality of service whether they are rich or poor. Under socialism, these class distinctions are eroded and replaced with people who all have a decent standard of life.

This is a fundamental point of struggle with capitalism which impoverishes social wealth under an avalanche of commodities – if you want to enjoy something you have to buy it.[108] The socialist alternative undoes the Lauderdale paradox of capitalism: that there is an inverse proportion between the existence of public wealth (common, social goods) and private riches. When a public library is closed and replaced by Amazon online sales, or when a beach is closed off and you have to pay to sit by the sea, someone is getting rich as your public wealth is drained away. Socialists prioritise access to culture, skills, free time and knowledge as the true wealth of a society.

This is the end of scarcity; or at least we can limit scarcity to that imposed by nature. We can produce food within planetary limits, ensure housing is available for all, and that human needs are met to allow us to truly flourish; as the US revolutionary James Boggs described it: 'for the first time in human history, great masses of people will be free to explore and reflect, to question and to create, to learn and to teach, unhampered by the fear of where the next meal is coming from.'[109]

Hierarchies Wither

By this point we have made clear that socialism is not what the state does, particularly under capitalism. Nationalisation, welfare, taxation, environmental regulation, all of these things are only faint echoes of what socialism will be. The modern right is so entrenched in its hatred of socialism that they regularly call even mildly liberal policies communist. They accuse US presidents who raise taxes slightly of being closet communists. They claimed that bailing out the banks in 2008 was a Bolshevik policy.[110] This is all just noise and fury intended to delegitimise socialism and make people feel hopeless about the possibility of a better world, while the powerful buy more super-yachts or private planes, living a lifestyle that produces huge amounts of carbon.

When reactionaries conflate an enormous hierarchical state with socialism they are confusing it with social democracy or Stalinism. The reality is that in a post-capitalist society where the market has been dismantled and replaced through planning, where exchange value has given way to use value, and where we are no longer divided into classes, there is less and less role for any kind of state structure. Socialists are not obsessed with the state, it is a necessary evil when abolishing capitalism; but we are champions of any gains that can be made when it comes to shrinking it.[111]

A state under class society is an instrument of class oppression and control, the state under feudalism protected the wealth and property of kings and aristocrats, the state under capitalism protects the wealth and power of the capitalist class and guards the nation state. Under socialism a workers' state and government will defend the majority working class and help with the transformation towards socialism. It will work to prevent counter-revolutionary activity and sabotage by pro-capitalist elements or other nations still ruled by capitalists.

No matter how much we try, the existence of a hierarchical institution like a state, even a workers' one which looks different and organises itself in a radically different way to the old capitalist one, is something that will feel external or imposing. The anarchists are not wrong to get rid of the state, it is just that they propose to do it immediately, whereas socialists believe that a workers' state will transform over time into something much less definite.

If we are successful in our struggle, if socialism becomes a global system and eradicates capitalism from every corner of the Earth then the role of the state becomes much less important. Engels described his view on this as follows:

> in the name of society – this is, at the same time, its last independent act as a state. State interference in social relations becomes, in one domain after another, superfluous, and then dies out of itself; the government of persons is

replaced by the administration of things, and by the conduct of processes of production. The state is not 'abolished'. *It dies out.*[112]

This follows similar views that Engels and Marx outlined in the *Communist Manifesto* about 'public power losing its political character'.[113]

We do not stop with the tools that we use to dismantle the master's house, we do not worship the concept of workers' control or a workers' state. As long as what we make and distribute is still commodified, is still paid for, and we work under a waged system, then we are living in a pre-history, a society still stamped with the birthmark of the old.

Some worry that socialism will mean endless meetings to decide everything, constant arguments and rows. Compared to the apparent simplicity of the capitalist market (turn up and buy things), who wants to spend their lives debating every point of human economics? This is, in part, a false argument, as a lot of production or economic activity will be automatic, based both on what we know people need and, no doubt, planning algorithms for some industries. However, it is the case that there will be more forums for discussion about managing society but this is because socialism allows for humans' genuine community spirit and collaboration to emerge as we self-actualise, as we collectively decide our own social needs.

The humans that will exist under socialism are not the same ones that existed under feudalism or capitalism. Socialists are firm believers that humanity is capable of understanding its own economy and making rational decisions without having to rely on captains of industry or the invisible hand of the market to decide things for us. As the law of value disappears: 'The struggle for individual existence comes to an end. It is only at this point that man finally separates in a certain sense from the animal kingdom and that he passes from animal conditions of existence to really human ones.'[114] Our humanity begins to reveal itself.

The Good Life

In an age of monsters, of violence and hate, where the clock appears to be running out for Earth being able to sustain humanity, it can be tempting to consider talk of humanity living a genuinely good life as a utopian fiction. Even some people who talk of building a better world fear in their hearts that perhaps it is already too late.

We have to reject this mindset. When it comes to society, humanity never sets itself tasks that it cannot solve,[115] and global warming is one of them. We can shift our society to survive on a hotter planet while also taking steps to return Earth to a more sustainable temperature over time. This is what socialism can do but capitalism cannot, because the power of fossil capital is too strong, too embedded in our world economy.

This fundamental hope is essential. But organising for hope is what matters.

When we overthrow the capitalist regime and progressively plan our economy and resources to meet human need, and the old class distinctions have withered away, then we will begin to approach a classless and stateless society where we can truly enjoy our lives as humans: 'In the communist social order there are neither landlords, nor capitalists, nor wage workers; there are simply people – comrades.'[116]

The ideal is to go back to what Aristotle described as *eudaemonia* – the good life. Such a world cannot *guarantee* happiness for all individuals always, as the Polish socialist

Adam Schaff explains: 'even in ideal social and economic con-ditions people can individually be unhappy – no economic or social system can protect them against disease, the death of loved ones, unrequited love, personal failures, etc.'[117] However, it can eliminate most causes of current *unhappiness*. We will have a society where our needs are met, what we do after that will be left to our creativity and imagination. It will be a society where all the old divisions and hatred have disap-peared. Women's oppression will no longer exist because the family unit, with women's unpaid labour at the heart of it, will have been fundamentally changed. Borders and nations will have been abolished; religious views that still exist will be a private matter.

As politics and economics are the categories through which we understand the struggle over resources, these separate concepts begin to fade into non-use as we produce enough for what we need. As society develops and there is no longer scarcity of what we need as dictated by capital there will be fewer *political* decisions to make. So what will replace politics? Perhaps just culture. But this is no longer a culture based on primitive social divisions and class differences but a genuinely human culture. Such a concept might well appear beyond our current imagination – but that just shows the potential for the world that we can create when we have overthrown the barbaric system that we temporarily slave under. We might just spend time discussing what the next community play will be.

This has profound consequences for how we feel as humans. Under capitalism, with its divisions of nationalism, gender, creed and class, scarcity, and therefore fear, comes to dominate and control. Capital can only exist by creating scarcity and selling to us what we need or desire. The fear of loss, of losing what few 'privileges' we feel we have over other people, comes to control us, to turn us against each other. As socialism is firmly established and we move beyond scarcity towards a world of sustainable abundance, these fears fall away. And with them, all the concern over crime, and the huge state apparatus that arrests and prosecutes and detains and punishes, and the armies that are formed to defend one nation against another, and the hatred of the foreigner and the immigrant. All of these neurotic impulses under capital recede into the background as we emerge out of the grim darkness of our pre-history into the new era.

By this time our entire concept of work has changed. We are no longer compelled to work in order to live, work is instead demanded according to the needs of the community and it is much easier. We no longer consider the distinction between work and 'free time' as if leisure is something clawed back from the economy. Our real talents can finally be explored without the constraints of needing money or constant work. Cooperation is no longer an unconscious and unrecognised way of being, it is now socially recognised, it is brought to the surface in an unmediated way.

Our time is no longer organised for the production of surplus value, or structured by the dictatorship of capital; instead the expansion of free time is the measure of wealth. The realm of freedom becomes the most important thing in our lives, not the crushing necessity of waged labour. A classless society is one in which we have abolished money but we are all wealthy. Everyone is rich in human experience, skills and opportunities because we have restored equilibrium with the basis of our wealth, nature itself. It is a society in which obscene riches for a handful of individuals based on the exploitation of billions is a forgotten memory of our pre-history, something for children to laugh about, how we used to live. One person living in private luxury will seem as distant and wrong to future generations as owning a slave does to us now. We are no longer the means to the end of power and money for those humans who own capital, instead the development of our human powers and capacities becomes the main driving force in our lives.

PART II

Debates

4

Arguments Against Socialism: Human Nature and Knowledge

The criticisms of planning generally fall into three, related categories: human nature; the theoretical argument around capitalism's superiority; and historical examples of how planning failed to improve society in the 20th century. This section will look at other arguments against socialist planning. It might be argued that a section dealing with human nature strays from the economic outlines of this book, but it is essential to argue against the commonly held view that capitalism somehow accords with the fundamentals of our human nature. The defenders of capitalism believe that their markets and institutions are essentially neutral and conform to what is natural in humanity; they ignore the role of ideology in forming our own consciousness. We also look at the socialist calculation debate, the idea that economies are too complicated to plan. Finally, we must look at the problems of the command economy in the Soviet Union, explaining how it was the lack of a democratic plan and workers' democracy which contributed to its ultimate collapse.

Is Human Nature a Barrier to Socialism?

The standard argument goes like this: socialism is impossible because humans are all inherently selfish and individualistic by nature. The human nature argument is a fundamental one for advocates of capitalism, because it is both considered the most obvious and because it strikes at the heart of the very essence of what is possible for us to achieve as a species.

Socialists reject this view of human nature. Human nature is everything that humans do. It is war but also peace. It is caring as well as hating, selfish or cooperative. Everything human is part of our nature, to claim there is an essential part which overrides the others *naturally* would need to be explained. Optimism and despair and everything between are all human traits. In contrast, the reductive view is that we are mere *Homo economicus*, rational actors motivated by narrow self-interest and competition. But are we really only that?

It is not that we have built an economic system that *reflects* the essential nature of humanity, it is that capitalism *encourages* the worst aspects of our nature. It exalts individual triumph over collective endeavour. It encourages us to ignore or deride the homeless and the destitute as lazy or unworthy because the capitalists require us to believe that hard work is rewarded. British Prime Minister Margaret Thatcher waged a vicious class war against the working class in a bid to destroy the very idea of collective solidarity or community. She saw the goal as creating a country in which there was 'no society, only individuals and their families'. She planned to do this through key economic policies that would shift people's consciousness, as she described in 1981: 'Economics are the method: the object is to change the soul'.[1]

If selfishness is rooted in our DNA then why is so much spent on ideological apparatuses of the media to reinforce this mindset in each of us? And why is so much spent on repressive forces to crush organisational expressions of solidarity such as trade unions or housing squats and other examples of collective endeavours that challenge the rule of capital?

Humans are capable of great feats of solidarity, energy, creativity and determination when they feel inspired. We have different personalities and psychological architectures, which is why we are capable of a huge range of behaviours, attitudes and actions. We also desire connectedness, personal autonomy and purpose. Our attitudes are socially shaped. In times of war, many people make huge sacrifices and even sacrifice their lives for a cause. The key argument for socialists is that our society is structured to encourage individual solutions to satisfy our basic wants and needs unless it is in the interests of capital. For instance, huge numbers of us work in the care industry. We can assume that the people working in these industries have a personal desire to look after people. But as a professional interest, this desire can only be realised in the form of a capitalist wage-relationship, to create profit for the business owners. Likewise, humans cooperate to build skyscrapers or dig train tunnels, to run schools and raise children.

Humans require their needs to be met, in fact they *must* have their basic needs met and they *deserve* to have their wants met too. In any type of society, humans have certain needs – food, clean water, shelter and so on. The problem is that capitalism cannot provide the basics for everyone in a way that guarantees security and happiness. If people want the best possible lives they could lead then the domination of capital will have to be removed from economic decision making.

Socialism is a practical consequence of the collective needs of humans and the importance of living in a sustainable metabolic relationship with nature. As a project, the aim of socialism is to transmute the individual 'selfish' needs of people into a reordering of resources and work for our collective good under democratic control by producers and consumers. But even if we start from the assumption that people will always ultimately act in their own interest, then that is still not a barrier for socialism. People's individual needs will be far better served in a world free from the domination and limits of capital because socialism will end enforced scarcity and competition for work and resources. A socialist system might be driven by self-interest, selfishness even, in some ways not totally different from capitalism.[2] After all, a strike over pay is usually motivated by people's personal situation (wanting more money), but they recognise their best route to winning is to have a collaborative struggle. Politically, that means building a mass movement against capitalism and for a political solution based on wider participation of the masses in seizing their own collective destiny.

Mass struggles are central because they demonstrate how humans *can* change their views and behaviour, and they change through the impact of society and the struggles that they wage, Marx recognised this when he wrote 'all history is but the continuous transformation of human nature'.[3] A collective struggle alongside others is a transformative experience, forcing re-evaluations of old ways of thinking and creating new social formations. The idea of struggle being transformative is a fundamental part of socialist politics. This is big difference from social democrats, who rely on opinion polling and surveys of already existing attitudes to determine their policies. The dominant ideas of any society are the ideas of its ruling class and this creates a social, intellectual and cultural framework that structures how we tend to think. But during any intense struggles ideas can change rapidly as people are forced to organise and confront existing power structures to assert what they need. The fight for communism itself is transformative, as Marx and Engels argued even back in the 1840s at the start of the socialist struggle:

For the production on a mass scale of this communist consciousness, and for the success of the cause itself, the alteration of men on a mass scale is an alteration which can only take place in a practical movement, a revolution; this revolution is necessary not only because the ruling class cannot be overthrown in any other way, but also because the class overthrowing it can only in a revolution succeed in ridding itself of all the muck of ages and become fitted to found society anew.[4]

It is useful to have a concept about how ideas are formed in the human mind. For this the work of Paula Allman provides valuable insights.[5] Allman outlines how human ideas are formed through interaction with the world around us and process the sensuous feelings through a thought process that is about the unfolding of internal relations. We receive sensory input (which could be anything from touch to reading a book), then these inputs are organised and understood according to a conceptual apparatus that is an accumulation of ideas that have developed socially over time. That doesn't mean that every human grasps the entire history of human thought, but that our society provides a way of understanding the world, through education, direct experience, institutions and ideology. Our knowledge as a social species is gained from the entire slaughter bench of history (as Hegel described it),[6] but our ideas, imparted to us through social interaction, are also changed by other material inputs. I might believe that the police are a force for good in society until one of them murders my friend or strikes me round the head with a baton on a demonstration.

This is where the idea of human praxis – actions motivated by ideas – is so important. Praxis is where our actions are intimately bound up with what we believe – the 'conscious shaping of the changing historical conditions'.[7] Allman argues that you can either have an uncritical praxis that merely reproduces the existing status quo or a critical/revolutionary praxis.[8] The social dimension to our learning is important here. We are not isolated individuals who exist outside of a society, humanity is social, we can only exist in relation to other people and that relation defines us. There is no such thing as a 'good theory but a bad practice' – if it is a good theory (meaning corresponding to socialist ethics and collective solidarity) then it is embedded in good practice and as such is realisable in the real world.

In the words of Allman, the fight for socialism means 'Marx's explanation of capitalism, his theory of consciousness (praxis) and the possibility of critical/revolutionary praxis when taken together, strongly suggest that authentic revolution requires the simultaneous and complementary transformation of both self and society.'[9] Ideas become a material force in the world when they grip the minds of millions, and so a clear ideological argument that emphasises social solidarity and internationalism is crucial to counteract the mass ideological framework of capitalism, which reinforces reactionary ideas of humanity. Understanding how human individuals exist as social beings within a class structure (also structured around race, gender and other forms of identity), and their social basis of consciousness, is an important argument against the view that we are all selfish or utterly individualistic.

The Supremacy of the Market and Profit

Let's look at some of the more basic criticisms of socialism before we get into a more substantial theoretical argument around 'socialist calculation'. Advocates of capitalism argue that only their system can create the conditions for truly rational economic decision making because prices send signals over how popular a commodity is. If you are making tins of beans and they are popular then you can guarantee money will be made, people will buy your beans. Competition with other baked beans manufacturers will establish the market value; if your beans are priced too high then you will be undercut by a competitor and be forced to lower your prices to something more satisfactory to the consumer. But the price of beans must also be judged against the price of a house and a car and deep-sea drilling equipment in that the value of everything is decided by the thousands of autonomous economic acts that take place every day. Money exists as the most realistic way to mediate these billions of complex economic calculations, it is an independent physical expression of different amounts of social labour.

Milton Friedman used the example of a pencil to demonstrate the beauty of the market. A pencil is simple and commonplace but to produce one (or millions) requires significant coordination between different companies often over international borders. Friedman and others from his perspective compare the vibrancy and dynamism of the market to the top-down, bureaucratic and wasteful production in the Soviet countries or the inefficiency of government and the public sector. In their mind, the whip of capital and competition sharpens human activity to a point of near perfection. This is the miracle of the marketplace.

Markets also function because of their simplicity for the consumer. You don't need to be involved in complicated arguments over economics, know how things are produced or spend endless time running the economy; instead, if you need something, you go down to a local shop or go online and buy what you need. The only information required is the basics – company name, price and possibly reviews to ascertain if it is a quality product. Your desire for a product drives intention to purchase, all the canny capitalist has to do is provide what you need.

The socialist calculation debate was primarily instigated by two Austrian economists, Ludwig von Mises and Friedrich Hayek. Their arguments are sometimes conflated but they are not quite the same. Von Mises has a calculation problem based on a lack of private property, whereas Hayek focuses on the lack of knowledge for ordinary people when it comes to making planning decisions.

In his criticism of socialism, von Mises makes the case that if there is no private property in the economy then you cannot set market prices for commodities; competition in the marketplace between privately owned goods creates prices that you can use for rational economic decision making. Without market prices you cannot work out any meaningful economic data, understand what is efficient, what is making a profit or a loss and so on. Economic rationality here means 'the problem of producing the maximum possible useful effect (satisfaction of wants) on the basis of a given set of economic resources'.[10] Essentially, rational economic calculation is impossible under socialism because in socialism 'every economic change becomes an undertaking whose success can be neither appraised in advance nor later retrospectively determined. There is only groping in the dark.'[11] From von Mises' perspective, the further an economy moved away from private property and money, the further it moved from any kind of rational economics. Without exchange value and market signals being sent (e.g. a company's profits collapse because they have released an inferior or unwanted product), all central planners can do is guesstimate on prices and quality. This would result in the 'the absurd output of a senseless apparatus'.[12] Of course, because of the bureaucratic nature of

planning in the Soviet Union, there were examples of senseless or absurd decision making, so that didn't help the socialist
argument. Von Mises sums up the logical conclusion of the
Austrian School: 'every step that takes us away from private
ownership of the means of production and the use of money
also takes us away from rational economics'.[13]

Hayek focuses on the question of knowledge, or rather the
lack of it under socialism. 'The knowledge of the circumstances
of which we must make use never exists in concentrated or
integrated form, but solely as the dispersed bits of incomplete
and frequently contradictory knowledge which all the separate
individuals possess.'[14] Essentially he argued (correctly) that we
do not live in societies in a static equilibrium, where there are
no changing variables – there are constant changes going on
which impact on production, labour, distribution, social spaces
and so on. Different people have different kinds and levels of
knowledge, and the marketplace is the best way to synthesise
that knowledge through prices (and prices form part of our
knowledge). If you want to buy milk you go to the shop with a
rough idea of how much milk costs, and if it is hugely expensive you don't buy it. This is the simplicity of decision making
based on the market. You don't need to know everything about
dairy production, transport and logistics, the economics of
supermarkets, wages or profit; you can make a decision based
on very simple information. Likewise, retailers or producers
who price their goods too high also get limited but meaningful feedback – for instance that they don't sell their products.

And, importantly, any planning that doesn't have market
signals is doomed to fail if there are significant disruptions
in society or economics. After all, in economic life 'constant
change is the rule' and therefore no central planner or plan
for prices can ever be as flexible or adaptable as genuine market-based pricing.

Essentially Hayek is a proponent of markets and capitalism because market signals have a simplicity and efficiency to them that cannot be rivalled. His argument against socialism is that it is too complex and, as such, unworkable. Socialism could only be attempted if it was in an authoritarian system where decisions are centralised (even then it would be done poorly). This is why he calls socialism the 'road to serfdom', because it turns us into peasants with no real power. Under capitalism he marvels at 'how the combination of fragments of knowledge existing in different minds can bring about results which, if they were to be brought about deliberately, would require a knowledge on the part of the directing mind which no single person can possess'. For Hayek, central planning empowers small numbers of all-powerful decision makers who are the only ones who have the information to manage economic and therefore political affairs. Modern-day liberal economists would point to the history of dictatorial regimes in the planned economies as proof that socialism equals serfdom, that it inevitably leads to the loss of democracy.

The argument that complexity renders conscious attempts to organise production redundant continues well into the 21st century. Joseph Stiglitz, who was a critic of globalisation but not capitalism, concluded: 'the central planner could never have the requisite information' to plan any economy.[15] Although socialists reject Hayek's most extreme pro-capitalist conclusions, his belief that markets remain crucial to economic decision making had a huge impact on market socialist ideas.[16]

Responses to the Socialist Calculation Debate

Before we look at socialist answers to the calculation debate, it is worth considering how the much-adored 'market price signals' that are apparently so essential for economic decision making are also incredibly limited. Socialist economist Richard Day makes the point that: 'The cyclical movement necessarily arises from the fact that today's prices, leaving aside speculation, are merely a "snapshot" of the consequences of past actions. Even more irrational is the fact that today's prices, in determining today's investments, also determine tomorrow's production.'[17]

What about the view that the profit motive is efficient? It streamlines production by forcing inefficient enterprises with worse labour productivity to the wall, which allows for the supremacy of superior companies with superior products. From the perspective of economists like Hayek and von Mises, the capitalist West had the profit motive that made amazing jeans and cool cars, while the blundering Soviet and Eastern European economies were making rubbish that no one wanted because there was no profit motive or market mechanism to incentivise better production of better goods. For instance, in the late 1980s East Germany was making the Trabant, famous for being a very poor-quality car (and even so had a huge waiting list to get one). Meanwhile, across the East/West divide they were producing the BMW 850, which looks better, runs better and had a more efficient production process, so you didn't have to wait five years to get one.[18]

It should be no surprise that the existence of the Trabant is not held up as the pinnacle of what socialism can achieve – in fact, on the superficial level, the pro-capitalist arguments are correct. It is a stereotype with truth in it that East German teenagers envied Westerners who had Levi Jeans and Calvin Klein products while they were stuck with badly made clothes and were less fashionable. Production in the command management economies was unreliable and wasteful, and the lack of consumer feedback, either through market mechanisms or democratic oversight, led to the production of worse and less efficient goods. Of course, this is actually an argument against the relatively backward system that was built under the *guise* of communism.

By contrast, however, capitalism is also hugely inefficient in how it works. Yes, it has transformed human society and lifted the living standards of billions of people, but it does so at huge cost. The American economist Stuart Chase identified four ways in which capitalism wastes both resources and human potential:

(1) the labour power used to produce 'vicious or useless goods and services'; (2) labour power wasted due to unemployment; (3) the unplanned nature of production and distribution of goods leading to inefficiencies and overproduction; and (4) the senseless waste and overuse of natural resources.[19]

Inefficiencies in market production can be seen all around us, not least in the huge amount of food waste that exists.[20] Under socialism, examples of waste reduction could include standardising power adaptors for smart phones and computers, saving hundreds of thousands of tonnes of waste a year.[21]

The market alone also hasn't played a particularly useful role in developing many national economies. Large parts of the global South remained underdeveloped for generations because there was simply no profit to be made in providing decent housing or infrastructure, but there was profit to be made from the extraction and plunder of natural resources. Some areas of sub-Saharan Africa have seen more development recently due to China's expansionist economic plans, usually as a result, not of the market, but of the Chinese state deploying economic resources to build hydroelectric dams and motorways in different countries (ultimately, of course, for their own benefit).

Some also believe that a free-market economy is the best way to allow the flourishing of individual talents and abilities. Only through the possibility of individuals getting rich from their own theories or inventions will new technology come about or new ideas enter the economy.[22] While capitalism has clearly allowed for a greater degree of human thinking and advancement, we have to critically examine whether the market is truly the best way of ensuring human genius can be rewarded. How many brilliant ideas never appeared profitable? Or were actively suppressed by existing capitalists to protect their own profit margins?

The belief in the supremacy of the market also provides a privileged position for those who already benefit from it. With so many people driven into exhausting wage labour just to survive, some living in slums without even the basics, can we really declare that capitalism has allowed all people to flourish equally? Most people who made it big in tech also came from either relatively well-off families or outright incredibly rich families. The basic point is that the libertarian pro-market myth of the individual genius in their garage creating a new product to get rich and relying on their own abilities and the belief that the market will successfully recompense them for their hard work is just that ... a myth. In reality, such a person probably only exists in a handful of countries that are already economically developed, has rich parents or a grant from a state institution and a network of people who can help get their product to market.

This argument also starts from a position of profound pessimism about people and what motivates them: that they only do something if it will make them personally richer. This is an incentive for many people, but that is because we currently live in a society that prioritises that view and way of thinking. But what about people like Tim Berners-Lee (the internet) Edward Salk (vaccines), Nick Holonyak Jr (LED bulbs), who all made pioneering breakthroughs that they didn't patent (Salk rhetorically asked a journalist 'Can you patent the sun?'). Most technological and bio-pharmaceutical advances also come from state funding, either grants to companies or from universities or government departments.[23] Even a global giant like Apple relied on state funding:

> Apple is a perfect example. In its early stages the company received government cash support via a $500,000 small business investment company grant. And every technology that makes the iPhone a smartphone owes its vision and funding to the state: the internet, GPS, touchscreen displays and even the voice-activated smartphone assistant Siri all received state cash.[24]

In the realm of pharmaceutical drugs: 'The US National Institutes of Health spends around $30 billion every year on pharmaceutical and biotechnology research and is responsible for 75 per cent of the most innovative new drugs annually.'[25]

Often capitalist companies will not enter into new and untested areas of market operations or product development without some kind of guarantee against risk. They have shareholders, after all, who will not like it if the company develops a whole new technology or product line which then flops. This is why so much of the private sector demands that the state underwrite its research and development; or enters into one-sided projects with universities or other public institutions to develop something which, if it doesn't work, doesn't cost them that much. The public sector absorbs the risks. Likewise, major infrastructure projects are always ultimately risk-protected by the state, even when a company delivers huge overspend several years late.[26]

These are general arguments against the supremacy of the market. When it comes to the socialist calculation we have to put forward a positive argument for how socialist democratic planning can overcome the market-supremacist criticisms. There are two points here; first, that consumption patterns remain relatively obvious as determined by population size; second, that large parts of the economy are not governed by fluctuating price signals but large-scale industrial units investing.

When confronted with arguments about how to manage a complex economy, Engels responded with a view that pre-existing patterns of consumption would form the basis for any future democratic decision making:

> just as one can easily know how much cotton or manufactured cotton goods an individual colony needs, it will be equally easy for the central authority to determine how much all the villages and townships in the country need. Once such statistics have been worked out – which can easily be done in a year or two – average annual consumption will only change in proportion to the increasing population; it is therefore easy at the appropriate time to determine in advance what amount of each particular article the people will need – the entire great amount will be ordered direct from the source of supply.[27]

He also argues that:

> In communist society it will be easy to be informed about both production and consumption. Since we know how much, on the average, a person needs, it is easy to calculate

how much is needed by a given number of individuals, and since production is no longer in the hands of private producers but in those of the community and its administrative bodies, it is a trifling matter *to regulate production according to needs.*[28]

Mandel develops this line of argument about whether the entire concept of the socialist calculation debate is misplaced in practical terms. After all, in any economy a lot of production is not for individual consumption but for clients, other companies, firms or parts of the state that order such things as equipment or services directly. Machinery and tech is often designed to specification based on agreed-upon plans for production. Once you strip out varieties of consumer goods, they are often the same kind of thing (bread, milk, socks, shoes, etc). This also affects labour decisions. Nurses and teachers are hired not according to random market signals, but data based on population size and a public sector plan for allocation of resources; the same goes for their workplaces in schools and hospitals. The idea that there are constant violent market price shocks and regular changes in consumption patterns is false. Prices usually change due to inflation, something that would be managed out of a planned economy based, in the first instance, on price controls (before de-commodification of goods). Consumption is mostly predetermined patterns and techniques of production that exist independently of any market price signals.[29]

Mandel concludes that if we look at the actual economic activity more objectively and see beyond the assumptions that there are infinite needs and wants that can never be properly allocated through a rational plan, then we might conclude, in fact, that the idea that every single economic calculation involves hugely complex decision making is an illusion promoted by capitalists who cannot understand the ways in which socialist democratic planning can simplify and stream-line production and consumption.[30]

How will prices be formulated in the early stages of any transition away from capitalism? In the 1930s, Oskar Lange and Fred Taylor developed the idea of shadow prices – in a transition economy you would initially price goods as if the law of value was still the determining economic regulator. Basically, the day after the revolution, keep prices as they are; but over time, as the economy is rationalised into a demo-cratic plan, the prices will be brought into line with the actual value of labour that went into each item (more labour goes into making a solar panel than a bike for instance). But the prices are only used for accounting purposes and, as we reach a system of plenty, we can remove prices altogether as we can properly de-commodify items and services.

Look What Happened in Russia!

'Look what happened in Russia!' is a common criticism that people use when talking about socialism or trying to escape the dictatorship of capital more generally. This is not a surprise, for 40 years governments calling themselves commu-nist ruled over almost one third of the planet. The Cold War between the capitalist countries and the communist countries was a dominant factor in politics, bringing the world to the brink of nuclear war during the Cuban missile crisis. A book on planning would not be complete without a clear explana-tion of what happened in Russia after 1917. After all, this was the first attempt by revolutionary socialists to create work-ing-class power and move beyond capitalism. Although this attempt did not succeed, socialists are not fatalists who believe that this means the entire cause is finished. We need to learn from failures as well as successes.

For the purposes of the arguments around socialist planning in this book, we will look at the main differences between how the Soviet economy was run and the kind of socialist planning we are discussing in this book.

Socialisation of Production and Distribution

Most of the states that defined themselves as socialist or communist rested on the socialisation of the economy. There were no private capitalists, instead a powerful state, fused with the ruling party, controlled the economy. The bureaucracy that took political control emerged as a consequence of the scarcity in Russia in the 1920s. After the revolution in October 1917, Russia was invaded by 16 foreign armies intent on crushing the fledgling workers' state. The Soviet state succeeded in defeating the counter-revolutionary forces but at huge cost, with massive economic destruction, and most of the passionate revolutionaries were killed in battle. The revolution survived but the workers' and peasants' Soviets that had led the revolution collapsed, leaving the revolutionary party to fill the gaps. Lenin warned in 1921 that Russia was 'a workers' state with bureaucratic distortions'.[31] He had also been absolutely clear that constructing a healthy socialism in Russia alone would not be possible, warning in 1918 that, 'the complete victory of the socialist revolution in one country alone is inconceivable and demands the most active co-operation of at least several advanced countries, which do not include Russia'.[32]

Despite efforts to support revolutionary struggles elsewhere, uprisings in Hungary, Germany and China were defeated, leaving the Soviet government in Russia internationally isolated. It was this specific historical context that led to the bureaucratic degeneration of the revolution as a dictatorship headed by Stalin took power. They turned their isolation into the theory of 'socialism in one country', that the Soviet Union could go it alone and that the strategy of communist parties in other countries had to be subordinated to the Realpolitik interests of the Soviet leadership. This culminated in Stalin agreeing, during the Second World War, to abolish the Communist International as a concession to the imperialists. After the Second World War the Stalinist state model was exported abroad by revolutionaries who still looked to Russia as a beacon for socialism, even after Stalin's regime had murdered countless revolutionaries in the arbitrary terror of the show trials in the 1930s.

This bureaucracy was ruled over by leaders who developed cults of personality to maintain their control. The rise of the cult of leaders like Stalin or Mao depended on the material conditions in Russia and China, namely that the chaotic nature of command management survived through a mixture of terror and personal fervour, and the propaganda of inspirational leaders who exemplified the determination of the masses.[33] The bureaucracy assumed control under conditions of scarcity, they could get you what you needed. As Mandel argued:

> So long as the exercise of certain social functions makes it easier to appropriate comparatively scarce goods and services, it is inevitable that the phenomena of careerism, nepotism, corruption, servility towards 'superiors' and an autocratic attitude to 'inferiors' will remain widespread.[34]

While the economy was socialised, it was controlled by unaccountable leaders and any criticism of the regime, or economic and social arrangements was considered 'counter-revolutionary', often resulting in serious punishment. One example of how the USSR was not socialist is that the bureaucrats running the plan focused almost entirely on output productivity, and not on a corresponding increase in living standards. Yes, lots of tractors were produced; yes, sometimes the targets for brick production were exceeded; but the workers still laboured away on often low wages for long hours.

What Impact Did This Have on Productivity?

What were the consequences of no participatory democracy in production? After all, you couldn't speak out for fear of being reported. This meant that the often arbitrary planning had little or no quality control and often appeared irrational in practice. You might fulfil your target of *transporting* bricks across the country but smash most of the bricks in the process.[35] Another example was the production of cookware, where the plan was measured in tonnes – this encouraged enterprises to make very heavy pots and pans to meet their targets.[36] In fact many outputs were measured in weight, which encouraged the building of bulky and heavy equipment and machinery to meet production quotas. By the 1960s, the poor quality of manufactured goods meant that four times as many people were engaged in repairs than in initial manufacturing.[37] As Mandel commented: 'From the point of view of the mass of workers, sacrifices imposed by bureaucratic arbitrariness are neither more nor less "acceptable" than sacrifices imposed by the blind mechanisms of the market. These represent only two different forms of the same alienation.'[38]

From the vantage point of people in Russia, planning helped to develop the economy considerably, rapidly industrialising Russia to the point of it being able to win war against Nazi Germany within the space of 15 years of the launching of the first five-year plan. Soviet institutions also made huge advances in technologies, including space travel and the atomic bomb, as well as education. But in a lot of 'state socialist' economies, including ones across the global South that were inspired by the Soviet Union, what the centralised planning achieved was to industrialise relatively primitive countries at breakneck speed – but failed to develop the economies into anything that could compete with Western capitalism.

After the 1950s, as the West experienced a consumer boom and sustained growth, the news from Moscow started to look more bleak. The planned economies suffered 'shortages of consumer goods; [an] inability to take full advantage of the world market for goods, capital and people; slow home-grown technical progress; and living standards that lagged behind those in capitalist countries'.[39] The inability to increase the productivity of labour is what ultimately doomed the Soviet Union.

While there were some changes in the social division of labour under the command managed economies, these were ultimately quite limited. The work done and wages paid were still deeply divided along lines of gender, and between mental or manual workers. The state retained the same oppressive, hierarchical structures as Tsarism (secret police, extensive use of prisons) and had no democratic input from anyone outside the fused party-state apparatus.

From an ecological point of view, the command managed economies were terribly environmentally destructive. In their rivalry with the West, they judged their successes on productivity, how many tonnes of iron ingot or coal could be produced annually, according to the targets. This led to very destructive practices like strip mining, and the lack of independent working-class or civil society organisations meant there was little pressure from below when environmental safety measures were ignored.[40] The explosion at the Chernobyl nuclear power plant in Ukraine was the most famous example of how the bureaucratic plan, with no accountability or democratic oversight, saw sloppy decision making and corners cut on safety, leading to the irradiation of parts of Ukraine and Belarus for hundreds of thousands of years. The drying up of the Aral Sea was caused by more land being set aside for cotton, alongside an insatiable demand for water. Massive canals were dug to syphon off the water, which transformed a crucial sea into a desert. All this was done under a 'planned' economy – pointing to the importance of ecosocialist politics as the basis for any decision making.

Why Did the USSR Collapse?

The socialist economy in Eastern Europe became stagnant by the 1970s. This was in part due to the massive expenditure on weapons that was forced on the Soviet Union by the Cold War and ensuing arms race with the Western imperialist powers. Supporters of the Soviet Union lay the blame for its collapse almost entirely on this, but we also have to consider other factors.

Alongside the cost of militarism was the massive cost of the bloated unproductive bureaucracy which had a fundamentally conservative view about economic improvements. The very structure of the economy itself militated against investment or dynamism. In a desperate bid to boost productivity, a series of reforms in the 1960s gave a much greater role to profit, though other market reforms were not introduced. The profits generated under the command planning of the USSR were set centrally as an agreed mark-up of a percentage of production costs. This meant that efficiencies in work would have reduced actual profit. If a product goes from costing 100 roubles to

80 roubles then the 20 per cent profit goes from 20 roubles to 16 roubles. There was no incentive for managers to introduce new technology or new labour techniques as this would have made everything more efficient and reduced profits, which the managers skimmed off the top.[41] Managers were temperamentally opposed to innovation or expanding lines of production because it would have impacted on the short-term managerial objectives on which they were fixated.[42]

The lesson is clear – the Soviet Union was unable to move past a primitive stage of socialist accumulation – it socialised the economy but failed to introduce participatory democracy or abolish the social division of labour. This is also true in China, Cuba and other countries that called themselves communist. The question of participatory democracy wasn't a 'nice to have', it was an essential part of the productive forces of a socialist economy, unleashing dynamism through innovation and quality control over output.

By the 1970s and 1980s, the sclerotic economy began to go into sustained crisis. Production targets were routinely manipulated or even outright ignored. Erroneous data circulated, leading to misinformed decisions by planners. The contradictions of a bureaucratic economy with no participatory democracy were mounting. Although wages were high, there were no basic goods in the shops. A revolution that had started by promising bread, peace and land ended up with bread queues. In this situation, Soviet leader Mikhail Gorbachev introduced a series of reforms to open up the economy, wrongly believing that a dose of market socialism would kickstart the economy again. Ultimately this led to its collapse.

Unwilling to be shackled to an oppressive regime, a number of states within the Soviet Union began to split away. Mass movements emerged in East Germany and Romania against their governments, calling for more democratic reforms.

Trotsky had predicted back in the 1930s that 'either the bureaucracy, becoming ever more the organ of the world bourgeoisie in the workers' state, will overthrow the new forms of property and plunge the country back into capitalism, or the working class will crush the bureaucracy and open the way to socialism'.[43] But decades of political atomisation with no independent organisations had left the working class with no strategy for wrestling power back and regenerating the socialist economy. This led to an influx of new leaders with outright capitalist liberal democratic politics, pointing to the higher quality of life in West Germany or the USA as showing the way forward.

Boris Yeltsin became Chairman of the Supreme Soviet of the Russian SFSR (the Russian Soviet Federative Socialist Republic) in 1990 and emerged as the leader of the openly capitalist restoration wing within government. The urgent need for reforms became wrapped up with the dismantling of any remaining planning; reforms became counter-revolutionary restoration. The victory of this wing led to a collapse of the economy and a decade of gangster capitalism in Russia, watched over by the IMF, which demanded total privatisation and the most extreme austerity measures imaginable to drive any last remnants of planning out of the system. A new capitalist class had to be forged:

> Individuals had to take possession, privatise property, factories, mines, wells, and forests. But since no one had the money to buy these state properties from the government, there was no feasible way this could be done legally, legitimately, or morally.… This class had to be hot housed, virtually overnight. And it was. In the end, a combination of elements of underground mafiosa, the nomenklatura, especially the top management of certain industries, and

segments of the intelligentsia – these people were essentially drafted to privatise the economy criminally.[44]

These parasites enriched themselves from the collapse of 'actually existing socialism'.

The lessons of Soviet Russia (and there are others for China, Cuba, Yugoslavia, but there isn't enough space to go into these here) come down to the importance of an international revolutionary strategy, popular democracy, a total restructuring of the economy towards socialisation and a democratic plan, and ruthless opposition to all entrenched bureaucracies and personality cults. Socialists should also be cautious of kitsch nostalgia: the hammer and sickle were a symbol from another time – any future socialist society will be built from the lessons of the USSR but not from an unreconstructed historical repeat.

Considering the difference between the Russian Revolution and the lack of revolutions in richer nations like Britain or Germany we can see the relationship between the combined but uneven development of economics, politics and consciousness. Trotsky made the point that in Russia, because the capitalist class was so economically weak it was also ideologically weak, and didn't have a strong ideological hegemony over society. This made overthrowing it easier. But because it was underdeveloped, the construction of socialism was that much harder after the revolution.[45] Comparatively, the bourgeois class in a country like Britain or the USA is much stronger, making it harder to overthrow:

> the richer and more cultured the country, the older her parliamentary democratic traditions, the more difficult it will be for the Communist Party to seize power; but the swifter and more successfully will the work of socialist construction be carried through after the seizure of power.[46]

5

Debates Within Socialism: Automation, UBI and Market Socialism

There is a tendency in this cybernetic age to grant information an exalted social role which it does not in fact possess.[1]

One of the main responses to the socialist calculation debate since the 1970s was that the economic inefficiency in the Soviet Union was because the technology just wasn't there to properly plan everything. With the massive expansion of computers and computer processing power since then many socialists now look to 'Big Data', tech and AI as the route to a socialist future. This chapter will look at the potential role for computers and tech in general under socialism. It is important from the outset to draw a distinction between what some are calling the automation debate (whether the automation of work under capitalism *inevitably* points to a post-capitalist future) and the role of automation, AI or UBI (universal basic income) in the post-capitalist world.

Technology and Planning under Capitalism

What technology exists under capitalism and how will it be used (if it is) under socialism? It is obvious that technology will be a central factor of any socialist society as we build a new world from the tools of the old one – we aren't proposing to go back to a more primitive time. But to what extent can we use planning or technology from the capitalist era?

Technology is part of the productive forces of society. For instance, Lenin argued that imperialism creates the basis of socialist planning because it forges huge monopolies that require large internal administrations to operate. Capitalist corporations make extensive use of vertical planning and computers for their operations on a daily basis. John Galbraith made a similar argument in the 1960s, that massive corporations are 'islands of planning', and classic capitalist notions of supply and demand are increasingly supplanted by corporate planners.[2] More recently, Paul Adler has developed this argument, calling for a repurposing for capitalist corporations along democratic socialist lines.[3] This theme was taken up in *The Republic of Walmart* by Leigh Phillips and Michal Rozworski, who point to corporations like Walmart as laying the basis for a planned economy.[4] The basis of this argument is that major international business like McDonald's, Apple, Amazon, Toyota and many others have long-term strategic plans as well as complex supply chains that all run according to a schedule. They have finessed methods of stock inventory and distribution using their warehouse and logistics systems. Data taken from websites like Amazon, crunched through modern AI algorithms, can produce accurate information for the kind of products people want. In this sense, it could be argued that planning is nothing new and, in some ways, not necessarily radical.

Cottrell and Cockshott, writing from the mid-1980s onwards, were proponents of using the latest computing power to tackle not just the question of processing data but also gathering it. They argued that planning consumer needs is 'feasible, using an economy-wide network of cheap personal computers, running spreadsheets representing the conditions of production in each enterprise, in conjunction with a national Teletext system and a system of universal product codes'.[5] They also used some pretty complex maths, which is beyond the scope of this book (that is, beyond my comprehension of the equations). Evgeny Morozov makes the point that what is really at stake in any economic decisions are two (related) issues: how to gather the information in the first place and then how to update the data with any kind of real-time frequency. That is far trickier than a more static view of how prices might be computed. Previous planning methods were reliant on the methods and technology of the time, with annual or five-year plans being very common; because these required a 'temporal closure', prices and investment had to be agreed on a certain date and that had to hold true until the next review period.[6]

Since 2020 there has also been something approaching a paradigm shift in AI technology, most popularly demonstrated by ChatGPT and AI image creation, but also within companies, a kind of revolutionary mathematics that has helped streamline production and distribution to incredible levels.[7] Inevitably this has led to anxiety over job losses (as the introduction of all new tech does under capitalism) but also hope that it can help with the complex task of socialist planning.

However, there is concern that the level of logistics and AI data work doesn't necessarily translate to the kind of planning necessary under socialism. Amazon and Walmart haven't solved the 'socialist calculation' problem because they do not use their immense operations to meaningfully plan *production*, only distribution. Following on from Milton Friedman's pencil example, Bjorn Westergard argues that if you order some simple pencils from the Amazon website, then the companies making the pencils still rely on the market to acquire all the raw materials. Embodied in each pencil is a multitude of private capitals working away – mining graphite, cutting down trees, packaging and so on.[8]

And sticking with this same commodity in his article 'How to make a pencil', Aaron Benanav also warns of the dangers of relying too much on computers and data to solve complex issues of socialist planning. Computer networks that gauge consumer demand could be connected to actual factories making the goods so that they can be made in the most cost-effective way imaginable, using the least resources required (an essential factor when dealing with environmental degradation). But what matters is democratic decision making over investments, not just consumer activity in the present: 'no matter how powerful the planning algorithm, there will remain an irreducible political dimension to planning decisions'.[9] Jasper Bernes has a similar concern:

> At stake in planning is not simply the question of whether or not all resources and all needs can be recorded and measured in terms of labour time or some other numeric marker, not simply the transparency of that data or its legibility in terms of a single measure. The more important question is about control – whether and how that measure can effect changes in the distribution of those resources in order to satisfy those evolving needs.[10]

This is true not just of technology but also the vertical planning of capitalist corporations – socialist democratic planning will be much more horizontal, based on popular control of economic decision making.

The danger of relying on accelerationist thinking about tech is that tech will not only replicate many of the social antagonisms and alienation that we have today under capitalism, but produce a kind of toxic post-capitalist variant of it: 'What might succeed is something no one would desire – a system requiring both surveillance and automatic coercion, a system which, in order to be efficacious, reproduces much of what we find intolerable about capitalism.'[11] We cannot ignore the drive by both Silicon Valley and the CCP (Chinese Communist Party) to use Big Data in an authoritarian way, ensuring compliance through mass digital surveillance. None of these technologies can be simply lifted and used wholesale from the world that created them. The fundamental point is that any new development of productive forces or techniques under capitalism is always geared towards one purpose, increase surplus value extraction from workers and maximising profits. Some of these tools we will no doubt be able to develop under an association of free producers and consumers, but we must be critically aware of how they are stamped with the power and economic relations of the old order. Just as we cannot take control of the state and just use it for socialism, the same goes for capitalist technology.

Cybersyn in Chile

When planning was more popular as an economic concept during the 1960s and 1970s, the first government to experiment with Big Data solutions was that of Salvador Allende in Chile with Cybersyn. This project has been examined in detail by Eden Medina, whose work is useful as a point of reference for the strengths and weaknesses of the approach. The Chilean left wanted to prove the efficiency of the democratic socialism of Salvador Allende, so the Chilean government hired Stafford Beer. He was a pioneer in cybernetic technology and an ex-business manager who had moved rapidly left, favouring a kind of decentralised socialist economics. When he was invited to be a consultant for the Chilean government, it was a huge opportunity to put his ideas into practice. He and his team developed a system called Cybersyn, standing for Cybernetics Synergy, which was intended to help the government have data-driven oversight of the economy.

The brief was to create a balanced centralised and decentralised, hierarchical and vertical method of communication and decision making.[12] It was based on two models, the Liberty Machine and a Viable Systems Model. The Liberty Machine would comprise separate operational rooms receiving real-time data, overseen by 'responsible officials answerable to constitutional masters'; that is, it was composed of 'a distributed decision-making apparatus of operations rooms connected by real-time information-sharing channels'.[13] This was modelled on the kind of war room that Churchill and the British military forces had developed during the Second World War, with maps showing the military operations and radio communications with area commanders to feed information back in real time.

The Viable Systems Model is something altogether different. It was overlapping and integrated systems which Beers liked to describe in biomechanical terms. System one was the sensory system, interacting with the second system, which was a kind of cybernetic spinal cord that allowed for rapid communication. System one, for instance, would be the workers on the ground carrying out the operations. System three was the cerebellum of the brain, monitoring and checking system one, the 'day-to-day management' of the operation. To measure and regulate voluntary and involuntary inputs and actions system four operated like the basal ganglia and the third ventricle of the brain, controlling the flow towards system five the cerebral cortex, the human aspect, made up of managers operating and communicating laterally, diagonally and vertically.

System three was how capitalist companies used cybernetics, in day-to-day and immediate operations. Beer's breakthrough was to consider how system four allowed for medium to longer term planning, and how that was integrated into system three.[14] System one operations could send signals direct to system five, the managers, through what Beer described as 'algedonic methods'. Beer intended to design a system 'to preserve factory autonomy and increase worker participation in management – the very values that set the Chilean revolution apart from that of the Soviet Union'.[15] The project even had an ambitious plan to gauge the mood of the population using the algedonic system, where each house had a dial in it for the residents to register their mood, between unhappy and happy.[16]

To a small degree, Cybersyn helped the Allende government survive the truck drivers strike of October 1972. The Allende government had announced the creation of a state-run trucking company to help deliver goods to more remote places, which suffered from lack of access because they were less profitable to service. This triggered a strike by self-employed transportation drivers who began a blockade of Chile's roads and depots. The opposition claimed this was a strike to defend the private sector against the encroaching 'socialist' public sector; in reality it was intended to be a prelude to a military coup.[17] Although Cybersyn was barely operational, it allowed the government to plan distribution of important goods and to systematise operations and decision making using masses of data. In this way, the strike was defeated, allowing the Allende government to survive for another year.

Despite its uses, Cybersyn was not able – nor was adequately designed – to change the structure of the Chilean economy; it was 'more a rhetorical than a practical success'.[18] As a reformist, Allende was keen to respect the principle of private property and saw socialism as an alternative economics that existed alongside capitalism – his government would not actually expropriate the Chilean capitalist class.

The cybernetics approach was condemned in the international and local press as 'Mr. Beer's Big Brother' – a system of surveillance and rationing that would destroy small businesses and lead to unprecedented government control of the economy.[19]

When faced with the reality of the totality of capital, and its oppressive practices embedded in the very productive forces of society, Beer himself doubted the ability of cybernetic state planning to solve the problem:

> if the final level of societary [sic] recursion is capitalistic, in what sense can a lower level of recursion become socialist? … It makes little difference if capital in that socialist country is owned by capitalists whose subject is state controls, or by the state itself in the name of the people, since the power of capital to oppress is effectively wielded by the metasystem.[20]

Medina emphasises that Beer detested bureaucracy and technocrats, and saw Cybersyn as a way of providing more freedom, not less. But his argument for the new technology was too fixated on the technology itself: 'By emphasising technology instead of Cybersyn's relationship to the social and economic goals of Allende's nationalisation program, Beer failed to definitively separate himself from the technocrats he criticised.'[21] This tentative move towards some kind of more radical computer-based system of planning was cut short by the CIA-backed coup in 1973. After the bloody coup, which saw socialists and trade unionists murdered *en masse*, Friedrich Hayek visited the country twice and defended the economic changes of the Pinochet regime.[22] Never forget that economics is about politics and politics is about power.

Automation and Socialism

Interlinked with the idea of existing capitalist vertical plans being used as a basis for socialist planning is the discussion around automation and digital/AI technologies already paving the way to a post-scarcity, post-capitalist future. There isn't space to go into all the arguments around this issue, but some key points need to be made.

One of the most popular socialist theories is that increasing automation under capitalism is forcing a fundamental change in the economy that will lead to socialism. Both Peter Frase's *Four Futures: Life after Capitalism* book and *Fully Automated Luxury Communism* by Aaron Bastani have this perspective. It is a vision of a world watched over by machines of loving grace where we have minimal need for inputs or decision making – the computers will simply do it for us.[23] Even Lenin and the Bolsheviks held this view to a degree, despite also advocating for Soviets as mass democratic organs of working-class power and decision making:

> Capitalist culture has created large-scale production, factories, railways, the postal service, telephones, etc, and on this basis the great majority of functions of the old 'state power' have become so simplified and can be reduced to such simple operations of registration, filling and checking that they will be quite within the reach of every literate person ...[24]

As we saw earlier, new technology taking jobs and changing the labour market is nothing new. From the Luddites in the English countryside smashing weaving looms in the 1820s through to industrial robotics and AI today in mega-factories like XPeng Motors in Shenzhen China which is almost entirely automated (though supervised by 600 engineers), the capitalists have always sought to revolutionise the forces of production to increase productivity and profit. As a result, since the earliest days of capitalism, people have been concerned that workers would soon be made redundant and replaced by machines that can do all the work for them. It is obvious that the nature of work has changed and many jobs have been automated, though new ones have emerged to replace them, but what is specific about automation theorists is that they believe that the replacement of human labour with dead labour (machines) is leading *automatically* towards socialism.

The central point to make is that although automation is replacing some jobs in some sectors the actual driver of unemployment is the over-accumulation of capital leading to declining profit rates which leads to de-industrialisation (as factories close down) resulting in jobs moving abroad, where profit rates can be increased through paying lower wages. In this sense, automation is only one aspect of this wider issue of over-accumulation.

The complex contradictory reality of automation under capitalism cannot be brushed aside by arguing for its full implementation under existing economic conditions as a short cut to socialism. The subsuming of living labour to dead labour (people to machines) can itself be an alienating process, consigning workers to 'increasing alienation, economic insecurity, and cognitive degradation', as Murray Smith argues.[25] There are also political economic reasons why the capitalist class will not just automate every function: new technology only gives a temporary advantage and once every rival company has adopted it, it drives down profit rates. This leads to an overall fall in profit and discourages new investment in technology, so then the capitalists turn to cheaper labour to exploit again. This obstacle mitigates a constant and never-ending drive for more robotics and automation.

In addition, not all work can be automated. This may sound like an obvious point but some of the automation theorists promote machinery and tech as if it will end the very idea of work itself. Social work and care work will require people, as will machine repairs, programming, teaching, creative work and so on. What we need is a focus on labour-augmenting devices. We can make teachers' lives easier with AI and new technology but it would be a dystopian world where children learn simply from robotic outputs on a computer screen with no human interaction. The same goes for healthcare or social care.

Technology under capitalism is often wasteful or harmful and is rarely 'value free'. There is also tendency for automation enthusiasts to have a dismissive or inconsistent view of the possibility of human agency to create revolutionary change. It is tempting to point to already existing technology which appears efficient, and to want to accelerate those tendencies, assuming that they will, at some point, become incompatible with capital and rupture the economic relations, creating something better. The danger with all techno-fixes or automation enthusiasts is what Mészáros highlighted, that: 'Unless some viable strategies of transition succeed in breaking the vicious circle of the by now catastrophic social embeddedness of capitalist technology, the "productivity" of capital will continue to cast its dark shadow as a constant and acute threat to survival.'[26] Certainly techno-utopians tend to downplay the environmental consequences of just growing the economy using new technology. The key argument is an ecosocialist one, that economic activity must be realigned within sustainable limits, rather than endless growth. The essential point is that while capitalism creates the *basis* for socialism, it also creates the basis for barbarism; unchecked, the constant drive to accumulate and compete is already proving to be utterly devastating. But it will not create socialism without conscious action by the majority to overthrow the rule of capital and the capitalists.

Universal Basic Income or Universal Public Services

UBI is a proposal that everyone gets a certain amount of money every month, whether they are in work or not. This would be paid for out of steep and progressive taxation on the very wealthy and big business. For instance, everyone in the USA might get $500 a month, regardless of their wage or wealth. This proposal is intended to help level up everyone's quality of life and provide a safety net that doesn't depend on welfare or benefit payments, which can be humiliating and are based on being unemployed or poor. In that sense, it uncouples the idea of a social safety net from your employment status – asserting that every human deserves a certain minimum standard to live on. It would also simplify complex social security arrangements into a single payment, which would help many people struggling with the often purposefully inaccessible welfare structures of modern states.

Some advocates of UBI see it as a key part of a progressive programme. Labour under the leadership of Jeremy Corbyn promoted a version of UBI. John McDonnell MP argued that it was an 'important contribution to the debate around inequality, austerity, poverty and ... a just economic system'.

Professor Guy Standing advocated a UBI model for the UK, arguing that neoliberalism has severed the link between work and pay, mainly because wages were stagnant due to weaker trade unions. UBI reasserts a universal right to life and living that directly challenges the belief that people need to languish in poverty before they get any state help.[27] Philippe Van Parijs and Yannick Vanderborght point to the reality of changing work with increasing automation putting people out of work – UBI can step in and provide money for people made redundant while also helping to create a steady-state economy that tackles the problem of growth.[28] One of the most popular books to advocate UBI is Bregman's *Utopia for Realists*, which makes the case that when given 'free money' people don't waste it but tend to use it to improve their lives in all kinds of ways.[29]

A system like UBI within a capitalist market economy can have unintended and negative consequences. UBI can be manipulated by capitalists to further their own agenda. Pilot schemes under capitalism can be used either to promote lives free from waged labour (what the left proposes) or to promote further privatisation (commodifying) of parts of the public sector by libertarians. It has been explored as a way of undermining the social wage, in essence re-commodifying public services by attempting to quantify what each service might be worth and then creating a price for it. How valuable is your local library to you based on how often you use it? What about healthcare? (US citizens already know the price of health care of course.)

As Brian O'Boyle points out, the danger is that UBI just cuts with the grain of neoliberal orthodoxy, inserting market relations and a cash nexus into our lives and rolling back the idea of a universal public sector:

Once a UBI became generally acceptable, it is likely that a neoliberal state would put major pressure on the provision of public services, in favour of opening up spaces for capital to profit. In a society that has already commodified much of the housing stock it would potentially be a trojan horse for the private sector in healthcare and education.[30]

Likewise, if UBI is to work it would have to be set at a level that was at a living wage, otherwise all it provides is a supplementary income, requiring people to still find work to survive. In order to get a UBI at this level it would require an intense mass struggle to redistribute wealth from the rich to everyone else. The issue is that you need powerful workers organisations like trade unions to force these concessions, which the advocates of UBI point out have been massively weakened by neoliberalism. So what is the social force that can force such a radical shift in wealth? And if it could why stop and redistributing income?[31]

Aaron Benanav argues that UBI needs to be more than a technocratic fix if it is to be emancipatory: it wouldn't necessarily help form social bonds eroded by neoliberalism, it would potentially foster reliance on the state (as the payer of the UBI) and does nothing to fundamentally change the relation between income and assets, allowing those in power to continue to enrich themselves from interest, rent and profit.[32]

There are also some important arguments against it when it comes to thinking about post-capitalist planning. Even if an advanced form of UBI guaranteed an income which frees us from commodified wage labour, it still does not deal with other crucial aspects of socialism, like socialising the economy. As Benanav asks, how do we wrestle the economy away from its owners, the capitalists?[33] The view of socialism put forward in this book starts from political struggles to massively expand the social wage, that includes socialising sectors like health, education and culture. It means a fight for the right to food, to assert that we produce enough of some foods to feed everyone and we should make them free at the point of consumption, paid for out of general taxation (in the first instance). These are reforms that can be fought for under capitalism that point to a world where the power of money and the 'price of things' is directly challenged. UBI doesn't deliver anything that radical, it would still allow capitalists and the state to charge money for healthcare and education, for the basics of life like food and housing, but they can justify it by suggesting it can be paid for out of a basic income.

UBI doesn't solve the issues raised in this book, including the role of the market in allocating housing or jobs. It could be seen as simply diverting a portion of the social wealth to buying off workers who are no use or of little value to capitalism: instead of libraries and healthcare give them what is effectively a form of government-backed debit card so they can carry on consuming capitalist products – a palliative measure. It doesn't socialise production or distribution, it doesn't promote participatory democracy and it doesn't really alter the social division of labour. But it does leave investment decisions in the hands of the capitalist class.

While Peter Frase and Aaron Bastani agree on automation as a route to socialism they disagree on the role of UBI. Frase sees UBI as essential to sustain people while robots replace them at work, but Bastani argues it would be economically unsustainable, and instead we should campaign for universal public services.[34] Expanding universal services not only creates more jobs, it is cheaper and more effective than simply giving people money. Such an expansion can occur under capitalism alongside a rapid and progressive de-commodification of both labour and goods and services under socialism during a revolutionary struggle against the existence of capital itself. The concept of public wealth as an expansion of the commons is more useful for people earning less money than UBI would be.[35] This means a struggle to seize control of the *production* of value and *then* its distribution, not a focus only on distribution.

Can We Have Market Socialism?

Following on from some of the arguments in chapter 4, the ideology and apparent simplicity of market socialism was appealing even to people on the socialist left – combining some public ownership and planning alongside a market regulation of production and distribution of goods and services.[36] As key parts of the economy remain regulated by the logic of markets, this means that the law of value operates and 'works its magic', ensuring profitability and expansion of productive efforts. *Voilà*, market socialism. The best of both worlds?

The origins of the debate about the role of markets and socialism began in the 1850s, between Pierre Proudhon and Karl Marx over the merits (or not) of a society of small artisanal producers.[37] Throughout the 20th century there was an argument for market socialism as a third way, between capitalism and command management economics. This started in response to the Austrian School debate (see chapter 4), with proposals sketched out by Oskar Lange in 1938. The problems of the command planning economies in Russia and Eastern Europe led to a renewed interest in market socialism. Internal market forces were reintroduced into Hungary and Poland during the 1970s in an attempt to boost production. The collapse of the USSR in 1989–91 seemed to be the final death knell for 'socialist planning'. These ideas of market supremacy also have to be seen in the context of wide-scale privatisation in Western capitalism and the rolling back of the public sector.

When it was published in 1983, economist Alec Nove's widely read book *The Economics of Feasible Socialism* became the bible for revived Western social democracy. It was published in the context of the growing crisis of the Soviet economy and the rightward shift of the European communist parties towards what was called Eurocommunism, a version of social democratic politics produced in response to Stalinism.[38] Nove's 'sensible socialism' was designed to salvage aspects of socialist politics while being more realistic about the clear supremacy of the market. He concluded in blunt terms that: 'In a complex industrial economy the interrelation between its parts can be based in principle either on freely chosen negotiated contracts, or on a system of binding instructions from head office. There is no third way.'[39]

Nove relies on the concepts of ex ante and ex post production: essentially, ex ante allocation is deciding what to produce ahead of time and ex post involves production for the market – that is, you realise if something was worth making only when it is sold. His argument was that ex ante allocation is always going to be too difficult to do in such a way that it will be superior to capitalism. Following from Hayek, Nove saw the Soviet economy as a tangled mess of hopeless complexity, that no rational plan or planners could possibly make sense of. A key problem was the Soviet party-state structure, both too big but also too small:

> The power of the state and the party is both too big and too small. It is so big as to prevent the emergence of autonomous and spontaneous activity, or free associations and organisations; it fragments and isolates. But it is itself fragmented, and has the greatest difficulty in ensuring co-ordination

of its own activities.... The system model assumes omnis-
cience and omnipotence, and many of its problems arise
because neither exists.[40]

If you cannot rely on an omnipotent party that knows
everything what can help with decision making based on
available data – prices? Instead, he argued that you needed a
dual economy, 'a system of binding instructions from planning
offices',[41] and then a second sector, dominated by the market
but subordinate to the 'planning offices'. Every worker would
work in a state-owned industry, a cooperative or an individually owned business. This was not particularly new of course.
Social democrats had been arguing for a mixed economy for
decades. During the debate with von Mises in the 1930s,
Oskar Lange argued for a decentralised economy of independent and competing social enterprises that set their own
prices on a guess-and-test method (guess how much something might cost then test if it sells). These operated according
to rules made by a Central Planning Board that would inter-
vene into the market, setting prices and encouraging demand.
For instance, factories would still have managers and could
charge their own prices, so long as the cost of raw materials
was set by the Central Planning Board.[42]

In Nove's model there are no large-scale capitalist enterprises, which is intended to keep the market economy more
flexible and prevent the emergence of a very rich capitalist
class, but there are competing enterprises all vying for market
share, which is meant to keep production sprightly and ensure
quality and cheapness. But this does not deal with the fact
that if one enterprise is successful and manages to drive the
others out of business, or buy them out or sabotage their competitors in some way, then it will grow and begin to take on
monopoly characteristics.[43] The bulk of workplaces would be

run by workers who would buy into an enterprise fund that would give them a stake in the success of their business. But, as each workplace or enterprise operates in a market, they would also be allowed to go bankrupt if they are inefficient or making things no one wants any more. Nove also believed that a socialist society would just see infinite expanding needs and wants. Because this was an unsustainable model, a market was clearly needed to prioritise allocation but also to limit consumption for the masses.

In fact, social ownership plus markets in many ways constitutes the dominant ideology on the left. More recently than Nove, Peter Rutland, in his study on the failure of planning in the USSR, concludes that it was the left's outright hostility to the market that led to disastrous outcomes:

> Far from maintaining a tirade against the market as the source of capitalism's evils the left should recognise that the market is in fact indispensable and should attempt to integrate it into their analysis. In the words of General Booth, founder of the Salvation Army the devil should not be allowed to have the best tunes.[44]

As the post-USSR crisis of the left rumbled on, some even looked back to Marx and Engels and found an argument for market socialism in the original texts, claiming that 'the "proletarian revolution" initiates a market socialism, albeit a state market socialism'.[45] Others, like David Schweickart in *After Capitalism*, argue for major structural reforms under a left government that could move beyond capitalism with only a few pieces of key legislation. He also proposes a market economy for goods and services alongside socialised means of production.[46]

Versions of market socialism are also bread and butter for social democrats, who see them as a form of mixed economy. They might also advocate for indicative planning – government agencies publishing targets for production – for instance the National Plan of the Harold Wilson government in the late 1970s. This created a framework for markets to operate under government supervision; the state becomes the head teacher monitoring the school yard to ensure fair play. At its height, the most radical vision of Corbynism in Britain was for a form of market socialism, though the Labour manifestos never mentioned the S word.[47]

Can We Have Socialism and Effective Market?

To some this seems reasonable, even practical. It appears to mitigate stifling top-down bureaucracy while allowing for a more democratic way of controlling the main socialised levers of the economy: workers' rights, alongside a limited role for profit making as a regulator to ensure sound economic development.

If you have reached this far in the book then it will not be a surprise to learn that there are some serious issues with 'market socialism' or any kind of socialisation of markets that occurs over the long term. This is not to say that there will be no shops under socialism or options for people wanting to consume, still, these are not real markets in a capitalist sense. As Girdin argues in 'Socialism for realists': 'Markets that simply accommodate choices are welcome to the socialist project but labour and capital markets, which undermine primary socialist principles, must be prohibited.'[48]

So why a prohibition for labour and capital markets? If we accept that price signals in the market are the only (or the main) mechanism for rational economic decision making, then this conclusion always leads to private property, profit and exploitation of workers. For there to be a genuine competitive market, there has to be multiplicity of private owners of capital. A market only exists because of independent *competing* formations of capital, and the market only 'works' as the dominant economic regulator by incentivising production through the profit mechanism. If we assume that an economy run by market allocation is superior to a plan of consumer production based on producer and consumer inputs, then we are accepting that anything distributed through the market has to be subjected to the laws of that market, including labour power and, as a result, wages.

This is the only way that an *effective* market can rationalise production.[49] Labour must still be commodified, its wages set by the pulsations of the market. Individual enterprises must be allowed to make profits, otherwise what is the incentive for operating in the market? Once profit is a central feature then the usual means of increasing it will come into play – lengthen the working day, speed up production, reduce wages and so on. These might be collectively agreed by workers' cooperatives operating in a market economy in order to outcompete rival enterprises, but then have we really progressed beyond capitalism?

And there cannot just be a profit incentive in a market socialist economy, there also has to be a *consequence* for failure. Enterprises have to go bust if they fail the cruel test of competition, otherwise there is no incentive to really improve goods and make money. Market socialists might reply that then the state can bankroll these companies or take them over under state ownership but this would end up fundamentally distorting the *necessary logic* of the market. Why have a market economy with a safety net that renders the market mechanism redundant? Without a proper market mechanism to allocate exchange values and therefore profits, you cannot properly allocate capital, as a workers' state will presumably prioritise social objectives over profit making.[50]

We have historic examples of this. A number of countries where large parts of the economy had been nationalised (by an admittedly undemocratic state), such as in the Soviet Union, Eastern Bloc countries, China or Cuba, resorted to reintroducing market mechanisms to try to revitalise their stagnant economies. These mechanisms included introducing profit margins and enterprise autonomy, paving the way for privatisation and the reintroduction of private property into the economy when the pressure from imperialist powers became more intense. They all lead to eventual collapse and reintroduction of outright capitalism.[51]

Worker Cooperatives

The problems of a market-driven economy would also extend to a model of socialism that is based primarily on enterprises run by workers' cooperatives. While it might be initially nicer to work in a setting where there is no managerial dictator and you and your workmates have a significant degree of control over what happens in the workplace, what is produced and so on, ultimately if the workers' cooperative exists within a market economy then the workers will end up dealing with a law of value dictating their wages, working time, effort and so on. Without a social plan of economic activity, they could end up suffering similar alienation and misery as under capitalist economics. The experience of the world's biggest cooperative, Mondragon in the Basque region of the Spanish state, is proof of this. Market competition forced the original members of the cooperative to expand to other operations where workers are on worse contracts, and less favourable terms and conditions, to ensure survival against capitalist enterprises.[52]

In a capitalist economy the workers' cooperatives have to compete with private sector industry which will use ruthless methods to undercut opposition and maximise profits. If a small farming or ceramics cooperative has to compete with a huge enterprise using the latest technology alongside intensive methods of production, it can be hard for the smaller workers' cooperative to compete. They have to sell their goods at greater cost and just hope that there is a market for 'ethically produced' goods, which might cost twice as much. In short, the contradiction is the belief that the market can be properly regulated when it fact it is the market that ends up doing the regulating.[53]

Before we go back to the issue of market socialism more generally, it is worth saying that if worker-run cooperatives were established in most parts of the world this would be an incredibly radical development, and anything that encourages workers to feel they can manage their own affairs is positive and can help foster forms of class consciousness. The general point is that confining the socialist project to cooperatives has severe limitations in the absence of a general social plan of production. Capitalism isn't the private ownership of one or even most enterprises, it is the totality of competition and profit and that is true even if most industries are run under workers' self-management.

Mutually Antagonistic Systems

Back to the central argument about market socialism, Catherine Samary describes the problem accurately:

> the basic idea of these pro-market reformers identified with socialism is that the Marxist critique of capitalism concerns mainly capitalist private property. In other words, in their

view it is the hiring of wage-earners by private firms which is the decisive criterion (which is why they propose stringent legislation on this point). Once capitalist private property is eliminated, or severely restricted, they believe criticism of the market as such is considerably less warranted.[54]

In other words market socialist (or even New Deal advocates) don't integrate the way the law of value operates into their view of capitalism. This can lead to proposals for economic models where, so long as the companies are publicly owned, somehow (either through workers' direct control, or popular shareholding) then the market relations are fine, perhaps even *natural*.[55]

As with worker cooperatives, it is important to not be dogmatic about denouncing markets initially in a transitional society, because the key point about whether a market exists under a transitional economy is to do with the stage of development. If you are moving away from capitalism, then to begin with there will still be a market for goods and services, just as there will still be money. Mandel was clear on this point, that the size of markets and the strength of socialist production exist in almost directly opposite proportions to one another:

the survival of the market categories in the period of transition from capitalism to socialism is primarily due to the inadequate development of the productive forces, which does not permit a physical distribution of all the goods produced according to the amount of labour furnished by each producer.[56]

If we accept that there will be a limited role for a shop merely as a way to distribute different goods expressing different preferences (different tastes of toothpaste or colour of jumpers), then there will exist some relationship between how quickly products are consumed and the information sent back to the production and distribution networks for more of them (or less). Bertrand Ollman and more recently, left-wing YouTuber Ian 'Vaush' Kochinsk advocated for a form of market socialism against free-market advocates as a *transitional* stage towards a socialist society. The question is whether there is a social plan of production that is progressively eliminating the law of value as the main economic regulator. But what this shows is the contradictions and mediations embedded in a post-capitalist transitional economy – it will not be a smooth and uncomplicated economic path.

One possible way out to reconsider the question is proposed by Pat Devine, that there should be a distinction between market *exchange* and market *forces*. A limited role for market exchange would allow for some useful economic feedback on various consumer goods. But what must not be allowed is the domination of market forces in decisions on investments. The priority is conscious planning ('negotiated coordination', in Devine's model) to decide on economic investment and expansion ex ante.[57] This would mean a shop where you could buy or select items you needed (depending on whether there was still a money economy), but the shop keeper couldn't change the prices. The 'transaction' would just be used as raw data for the production units to decide whether more or less of that item was needed.[58]

Connecting this back to the socialist calculation debate, Devine's model has been challenged by Max Grunberg, who argues that these are essentially pseudo-market forces that are only possible if you have fixed prices for everything, and any problems that had to resolved by negotiated coordination would require impossible amounts of workers' and consumers' knowledge all along the supply chain (here we can see

Hayek's challenge concerning knowledge reappearing).[59] Grunberg is generally critical of models of socialism that seem to emphasise either countless meetings or require near impossible levels of participation around identifying individual needs in order to inform production, 'It is more than comical how the emancipatory politics of conscious control collapses here in a collective agony of meticulously completing wish lists at regular intervals that would be comprised of several million entries at least.'[60] Grunberg proposes the use of AI to assist with planning for consumer items, as the forecasts could be made accurate with consumer data – freeing up time for people to make decisions on the bigger questions around social investment.

Ultimately, the proposal for collectively owned production alongside a marketplace which *determines* distribution is unworkable. It forces together antagonistic and incompatible political and economic systems and assumes they complement each other. Essentially you would have a mode of distribution that would come into conflict with the mode of production, or you would have to allow the mode of distribution (market forces) to restructure the wider economy to ensure it actually functioned, reintroducing capital, private property, risky investments and blind production of commodities – all the things socialism is meant to be overcoming. It would mean that the surplus produced by society would be guided by the tyranny of the market instead of being collectively controlled.

As an example of where it would go wrong, we can imagine how independently run companies end up competing, duplicating work or creating waste:

If twenty steel producing plants across the country in a market socialist system see that steel is selling well above cost and hence decide to invest double their capacity to reap large profits on the invested capital, the market will be flooded, steel will no longer sell above their cost, the investor collectives will not realise the goal they invested for and society will have wasted resources.[61]

Profit motives can drive efficiencies up to a point, but they can also cause waste which is something an ecosocialist society would, on principle, avoid. In short, the ruthless competitive elements that make markets work are antithetical to socialist society and any attempt to ameliorate them would be antithetical of the functioning of the market.

6

Green New Deal, Ecosocialism and Degrowth

The climate- and ecological crisis can no longer be solved within today's political and economic systems. That's not an opinion. It's just simple maths.

Greta Thunberg

Looking at the way capital exists and accumulates no matter the cost, we can safely conclude that capitalism is a death cult. It is a cult because it cannot reason or reflect outside of itself, and all the attempts to 'correct' or 'adapt' it only represent continuations of the existing ideological thinking.[1] Liberal institutions like the UN launched their Intergovernmental Panels on Climate Change (IPCCs). Accords have been signed in Kyoto (1995) and Paris (2016). The Conference of Parties (COP), which is meant to review the implementation of the UN Framework Convention on Climate Change meets annually. Companies have changed their logos to green and committed themselves to more and more spending on environmental research and design. Governments declare climate emergencies. And yet …

It is widely reported how wasteful the richest 1 per cent of people on the planet are. *Bloomberg* reported in 2022 how the small number of people on the planet in the top percentile (the more than 60 million people earning $109,000 a year) were the fastest-growing source of emissions.[2] Their lifestyles contribute over 15 per cent of all greenhouse gas emissions.[3] But it isn't just about rampant pollution by wealthy individuals, it is about the system of capital and its contribution to planetary ecocide. The Carbon Disclosure Project reported in 2017 the 100 companies that contributed the most to greenhouse gas emissions – 71 per cent of the total. It goes without saying that the top ten polluters were all petrochemical or fossil fuel companies; China Coal 14.3 per cent, Saudi Aramco 4.5 per cent, Gazprom OAO 3.9 per cent, National Iranian Oil Co. 2.3 per cent, ExxonMobil Corp. 2.0 per cent, Coal India 1.9 per cent, Petróleos Mexicanos 1.9 per cent, Russia Coal 1.9 per cent, Royal Dutch Shell PLC 1.7 per cent, China National Petroleum Corp 1.6 per cent.[4] It is worth pointing out as well that the company with the most emissions is Saudi Aramco if you start from 1965; China Coal is a relative newcomer onto the block by comparison.

As the ecologist Michael Mann said:

> The great tragedy of the climate crisis is that seven and a half billion people must pay the price – in the form of a degraded planet – so that a couple of dozen polluting interests can continue to make record profits. It is a great moral failing of our political system that we have allowed this to happen.[5]

The record profits are the reward for fuelling fossil capitalism, for providing the raw material for energy so that capitalism can function and grow.

And it isn't just companies. The military-industrial complexes of the powerful imperialist nations are also hugely environmentally damaging. The US military revealed in 2017 that it was burning through 269,230 barrels of oil a day.[6] Indeed, one of the reasons why the USA never ratified the

Kyoto Protocols is because it 'threatens to limit the exercise of American military power'.[7] Capitalism, operating in distinct nation states with competing interests, does not have the tools to fix the problem. None of the international treaties on the environment (except for the Kyoto Protocols from 1997) are binding in a meaningful way. This means that heads of state visit the COP meetings, speak positively at press conferences about new international agreements and then return to their capital cities to flagrantly ignore them. Even when the capitalist class turn their attention to the problems of environmental degradation, they invariably end up using capitalist methods to fix them, for instance carbon credits, cap and trade, or the EU moving 'toward cross-border taxes to promote compliance with global agreements'.[8] Even the much vaunted Paris Agreement of 2015 focuses on making renewable energy 'competitive' by 2050, still trapped in the death cult logic of capital accumulation and market share value. They cannot see beyond their own system – and why would they?

Red-Green Thinking

Alternatives are urgently needed. In opposition to the death cult and reactionary solutions provoked by concerns about overpopulation there is a rejuvenated socialist debate on post-capitalism. There have been important shifts in socialist thinking in the last few decades. One of the key changes in the discussion of what a possible future socialist society might be like is the turn towards ecosocialism. Previously, many socialists had a one-sided view of productivism as a good thing in and of itself. They saw the environmental movement as a bunch of 'middle-class crusties' and were even antagonistic towards them. For their part, the green movement would point to Chernobyl or the devastation of the Aral Sea in the 'socialist' states as evidence that the left didn't care about the environment.[9]

Roughly speaking, until the 1990s, a socialist society was usually talked about in terms of massive expansion of the productive forces, creating a society of plenty that could be enjoyed by everyone and not just wealthy Westerners. Socialists, of course, weren't blind to the concerns about the impact of rampant consumerism on the planet, but the pressing issue of overcoming the carbon-based economy and preventing global catastrophe was often not yet a central feature of socialist thinking. Ernest Mandel, in his book *Marxist Economic Theory* from 1965, argued: 'A fresh powerful expansion of the productive forces is thus indispensable in order to ensure an abundance of industrial goods for all the world's inhabitants. This expansion undoubtedly requires a doubling, or even a trebling, of present-day world industrial production.'[10] The notion that the productive forces must be qualitatively expanded is what is challenged by ecosocialism. Today we would be more cautious, or perhaps more considered about what that would look like. The *Ecosocialism Manifesto* from 2001, written by Joel Kovel and Michel Löwy, defines this as 'first-epoch socialism', which was then followed by the second epoch, ecosocialism, which 'retains the emancipatory goals of first-epoch socialism, and rejects both the attenuated, reformist aims of social democracy and the productivist structures of the bureaucratic variations of socialism'.[11]

More recently, the idea of degrowth economics, or even a form of degrowth communism, has been developed which explicitly criticises the notion of capitalist growth and considers ways to reduce economic activity as a strategic goal to reduce energy usage and environmental degradation.[12] Declarations have been issued from ecosocialist conferences in Belem and Lima that represent calls to action for mass movements of resistance.[13] There have also been renewed calls for a New Deal, this time a Green New Deal, the proposals of which usually swing between radical green social democracy and green capitalism.

Some socialists have taken to using the geological phrase 'the Anthropocene', meaning the era in which humans have most impacted their environment through new technology that has fundamentally altered nature. Others have rejected this term as too technologically determinist and more in keeping with the natural sciences than any Marxist under- standing of history as class struggle.[14]

Do We Need Degrowth? (Or, Stop the Treadmill I Want to Get Off!)

A major argument within socialist circles concerning post-capitalist economics is over the strategy of degrowth. The argument against endless capitalist growth focuses on the problem of GDP as the primary measure of economic progress and calls for a qualitative transformation in societal relations, alongside a quantitative reduction in economic activity (e.g. a reduction in economic *throughputs* in parts of the economy such as carbon emissions, plastics, etc.). This would create a greater focus on sustainable economics.[15]

These arguments are not new; an emphasis on criticis- ing infinite growth on a finite planet first became popular in *The Limits to Growth* in 1972.[16] The word degrowth comes from the French *décroissance*, meaning reduction, which has been part of the environmental movement in France for many decades. With the climate crisis now very real and immedi- ate it has taken on a renewed vigour as a political framework. These arguments challenge what some call 'the treadmill of production', an ideology that unites 'corporations, the state, and labour [who] are all committed to economic growth, with this "ideology of growth" having dominated both capitalist and socialist societies in the twentieth century'.[17] The degrowth argument could be positively summarised as follows: 'Ecosocialist degrowth signals a new civilisation that breaks with productivism and consumerism, in favour of shorter working time, thus more free time devoted to social, political, recreational, artistic, ludic, and erotic activities.'[18]

The framing of the problem as one of 'growth' is the movement's strength, but also its weakness. It is a strength because it has burst the bubble that GDP should be the primary measure of humanity and poses questions that capital will struggle to solve (though some degrowthers, such as Serge Latouche, think it is possible with capitalism). It points to the problem of endless accumulation as a good thing in itself. But it is also a weakness because, on the surface, it can be taken to largely focus on the quantitative aspect – sheer economic throughput – and less on the substantive, qualitative question of what is being produced. Likewise, there have been criticisms from activists in the global South about the degrowth argument: simply put, 'Degrowth is not appealing in the South because the reality there is that their ecological footprint is still low and the basic needs of the population have not yet been met.'[19]

From the degrowth perspective, Jason Hickel proposes a different way to consider degrowth, that it:

is *not* about reducing GDP. It is about reducing the material and energy throughput of the economy to bring it back into balance with the living world, while distributing income and resources more fairly, liberating people from needless work, and investing in the public goods that people need to thrive.[20]

However, if it isn't about reducing GDP then it seems strange to fixate on degrowth as a *strategic* economic goal or endpoint. Nevertheless, as we have seen, a lot of the concepts of degrowth coincide with, or are even drawn from, general ecosocialist politics so there is no need for a polemical rejection of the core ideas.

Outside of discussions over the specifics of whether the economic output is growing or not and on what basis, we have to consider the politics of mass mobilisations as well. The problem with degrowth as a rallying slogan is that it implies something somehow worse, something lesser than what we have at present. Of course, it might be the case that, with serious environmental breakdown, rationing is introduced, even under socialism, but this isn't a concept that will mobilise the mass of workers and urban poor to take action – until it is too late. Jonathan Neale's *Fight the Fire* argues we must fight poverty first, before we talk about any kind of structural degrowth, otherwise you cannot mobilise the forces needed to achieve an ecosocialist society. The economist Joseph Stiglitz has also challenged the no-growth logic, because to stop growth would not reduce carbon emissions, it would only halt them at their current unsustainable levels. In addition, 'The "no growth" argument diverts attention from the key issue of breaking the relation between consumption and production on the one hand and destruction of the environment on the other.'[21]

The question of how and what to 'degrow' can only be approached from specifics. When we talk about reducing economic activity then it is specific areas that must be identified – petrochemicals, defence spending, unnecessary plastics, deforestation, forms of industrial mass fishing and so on. As an example, abolition of the US military-industrial complex would remove a huge amount of wasteful carbon emissions and help reallocate resources towards socially useful activity.

The contradiction is that 'while the Earth has biophysical constraints, social demands are potentially limitless'.[22] Perhaps a focus on the positives – a low-carbon economy, a society based on rational planning of resources, one of genuine equality and equity – is a better way to conceptualise the future than 'degrowth', even if a key strategic goal is shrinking or ending parts of the economy that are wasteful or carbon intensive. However, electricity is one of the main issues in debates within the left over whether degrowth is needed, that is, whether we can maintain our current energy consumption but make it green or whether we need to massively reduce consumption. One perspective is to look at what level we are looking for when we work out averages for energy consumption. John Bellamy Foster has suggested that a reasonable level of energy consumption for every human is equivalent to the average Italian citizen's consumption in a year.[23] But there can be problems basing it on individual use as a socialist economy will prioritise collective public goods (like libraries and gyms) that all people can use.

It goes without saying that any reductions in economic activity must occur within the context of reducing global inequality. In a future global socialist society, many parts of the planet will still need significant improvements: better roads, more schools, quality foods and so on. There will still be economic activity that produces greenhouse gases, though it should be significantly lower than under capitalism. Meanwhile, in the developed nations, there are carbon-intensive luxuries that can and must be reduced dramatically. In 2022, the International Energy Agency reported that 775 million globally did not have access to electricity. This was an increase of 20 million from the year before.[24] In the Democratic Republic of Congo, ravaged by war driven by extractive capitalism, only 13.5% of its population have access to electricity. Any recalibration of the global economy has to lift the lives of the many millions that capitalism has abandoned and cannot profitably bring out of poverty.

Under capitalism, the price mechanism is relied upon to limit supply of what might be considered dangerous commodities or activities. A green capitalism might well see plane flights increase dramatically in cost in order to prevent mass consumption. But, of course, they will still be within the financial reach of the wealthiest, merely replicating inequality of living standards and consumption but under a green banner.

Benanev points out that investment will still be necessary, even in a degrowth or static state society, one which has decided not to expand its *overall* economic throughput.[25] Investment doesn't necessary add to the economic throughput overall. For instance, with a focus on improvement, Saito argues that important institutions like universities do not need GDP growth of 3 per cent a year, they just need to improve education and the learning experience.[26] The same goes for theatres and sports arenas. And the specific contours of a planned shift towards a low-carbon economy can be seen as an opportunity in the global South. After all:

it is not necessary 'or possible' for the 'developing' countries to achieve the patterns of individual ownership of consumer goods as exist in the imperialist countries: they have the possibility to 'leap over' this stage and move directly to more collective consumption patterns.[27]

Even on the basis of seeking meaningful equilibrium between North and South, East and West, developed and underdeveloped, it is doubtful, in the stage of socialism, that a society of abundance such as we have in some countries under capitalism will exist. One of the key arguments needed to win a socialist future is to reconceptualise what it means to live a meaningful life, or one of happiness. It can no longer be linked to near endless consumer goods, or the cult of luxury items as a marker of success as a human being. But neither can socialism be a society of cold, misery and austere Spartan deprivation. Some who are concerned about environmentalism promote small-scale food production as an alternative to mass industrial farming ('small is beautiful').[28] The practical problem with this is that billions of people on the planet live in cities and large towns that cannot sustain themselves from growing food in their gardens. To depopulate cities is a reactionary project, just as forcing everyone to become a small-scale farmer is simply unworkable.

The rise of the Green New Deal (GND) strategy is an important development in attempting to mainstream environmental policies. There is a reformist version of this – it is often pursued as a left position within existing social democracy or liberal parties, a package of demands such as insulated housing and free public transport. Others see the GND as a more revolutionary approach – a set of demands for a mass movement to mobilise around and not just to lobby politicians. Even then, GND policies often end up as a form of market socialism – a kind of Keynesianism plus elements of workers' management. More mainstream GND advocates promote their policies as in some ways beneficial for some capitalists (more investment, more subsidies, etc.), while also being positive for workers and the environment. The ideas of the GND are usually pitched as a policy for a government in parliament, not a radical rupture with capital using revolutionary methods. Some elements of the GND have been criticised for failing to break from productivism, that it greens the treadmill but the treadmill remains. The market socialist elements of the programme would suffer the same problems as described earlier (pp. 189–93). There are also credible accusations of green extractionism and dangers of a neocolonial approach as social democrats in the West propose sucking resources out of the global South to power energy production in the North.[29] As long as value form production dominates the economy, all talk of a new deal is only a variation of green capitalism. Workers' control of industry only changes the legal form of ownership of the means of production, it does not alter the basis of commodity production unless a democratic social plan rapidly and progressively eradicates the law of value.

There is a danger that some argue for a technology to solve the problems, believing that new tech will somehow unlock the future. We looked at the problems with this view in chapter 5, but it is also worth adding that this political trend can also lead to a kind of Promethean thinking, that humanity can 'bestride the world like a mighty colossus' and reshape everything from mountains to the eco-sphere according to our designs. This Promethean thinking has been challenged by socialism throughout its history, however, including by Engels who warned:

> Let us not ... flatter ourselves overmuch on account of our human conquest over nature. For each such conquest takes its revenge on us. Each of them, it is true, has in the first place the consequences on which we counted, but in the second and third places it has quite different, unforeseen effects which only too often cancel out the first.[30]

Even in the early Soviet Union, leaders like Bukharin were concerned with Promethean thinking; 'man can never escape from nature, and even when he "controls" nature, he is merely making use of the laws of nature for his own ends'.[31] Given these early principles, it is a tragedy that the rise of the counter-revolutionary bureaucracy led to such huge disregard for the climate and environment.

Against the productivist Promethean thinkers who praise the constant growth of productive forces (alongside new tech) without considering their impact on our planetary limits, ecosocialists have to counterpose the vision of communism as the realignment both of humanity with itself and with nature. This isn't to idealise a return to a more idyllic past, when humans barely impacted on the planet but also lived short lives with no medicine or modern conveniences. It is to say that capitalism, as the forced division of humanity through the universal domination of capital and its manifestation as private property, must be overcome; a new society must arise from the old, from which we take the best but leave the worst behind. Marx wrote eloquently about this in 1844, as he was thinking through his own radicalisation, about what it meant to be a communist, and a future where:

> communism, as fully developed naturalism, equals humanism, and as fully developed humanism equals naturalism; it is the *genuine* resolution of the conflict between man and nature and between man and man – the true resolution of the strife between existence and essence, between objectification and self-confirmation, between freedom and necessity, between the individual and the species. Communism is the riddle of history solved, and it knows itself to be this solution.[32]

Ecosocialism as an Alternative

Now the question has become more central: how can social-ism as a planned economy help to halt or even reverse global warming and destructive climate change? The urgent need to create a mass ecosocialist movement is inevitably held back by the ideological baggage of capitalism. The problem is that capital is so ubiquitous, and we rely on it to provide wages to live; that many of us feel invested in the system as it is, and are certainly wary of systemic change if it might threaten industries that provide well-paid jobs or impact on our life-styles in any meaningful way. An international survey in 2021 found that many people in Western countries believed they were already doing a lot to combat global warming, but felt that corporations and their governments were doing far less – pointing to a desire for structural and not individual changes.[33] Certainly the obstacles to winning people over to an ecoso-cialist plan include challenging corporations pushing 'lifestyle changes' or fake solutions like carbon offsetting, but also the politics of scarcity that drive fear and reaction. For instance, an ecosocialist plan means replacing polluting cars with expan-sive and free public transport, not just taxing people out of car use. We must also resist any politics of 'tackling climate change' that involves public borrowing and then austerity cuts to the public sector – again the false choice between funding healthcare and preventing further environmental collapse must be challenged.

A socialist society will have the democratic mechanisms to decide on levels of consumption that meet human need, ensuring a good standard of living within sustainable envi-ronmental parameters. A necessary stage of breaking down capitalism and introducing socialism is to sever the dual aspect of commodities – no longer will they be both exchange values and use values. Increasingly they will be seen only as use vales, what they are directly useful for. We might add also, as William Morris points out that everything should be useful *and* beautiful, that as much as possible of what we make should be aesthetic and pleasurable.

This means tackling the manufactured wants caused by the rapacious desire for profit. Advertising is one of the largest global industries; spending in 2022 was $1.568 trillion.[34] An ecosocialist society will do away with advertising, which exists to create manipulated needs and replace it with genuine information about goods and services. Such platforms already exist under capitalism, with consumer reviews on websites, but it would be better to have consumer associations with some social credibility to ascertain the quality of goods.[35]

The alienation of class-based society is found not just between humans but between humans and nature. The fact we conceive of ourselves as somehow separate from it or totally superior to it (because we are conscious) is part of the problem. The superiority leads to dangerous views that we can dominate nature, just as the capitalist class feel it is their birthright to dominate the rest of us. Part of the shift in consciousness that is needed is not just class consciousness, but a class consciousness that is rooted in solidarity with the planet. Workers and the environment are degraded, abused and exploited by the capitalist class, the conscious human part and the unconscious 'natural' part; Ollman describes it as 'becoming conscious of the internal relations between what are today called "natural" and "social" worlds, and treating the hitherto separate halves as a single totality. In learning about either society or nature, the individual will recognise that he is learning about both.'[36]

The key shift in consumables will be that there will be fewer disposable and low-quality items. Our landfills are full of consumer items that will never organically break down, the product of a buy-cheap-and-discard-quickly society. Reducing the sheer quantity of consumer goods made, and focusing on fewer items that are better quality and more durable, will be a huge benefit to managing our resources and slowing down environmental degradation. It is telling that one of the break-throughs in capitalist marketing in recent decades has been to make consumer goods that have built-in (planned) obso-lescence, like mobile phones that degrade in battery and processing power more quickly, forcing the owners to buy a new one. Or goods that have non-fixable parts that require you to buy an entire new product as opposed to making a simple repair. Another example of how capitalism prioritises profit over good sense.

So a Marxist conception of abundance is one of plentiful use values, not exchange values – directly useful consumer goods that are not produced for their profitability but for how much they satisfy human needs. Importantly, when it comes to calculating production costs there will be no more exter-nalities – the environmental impact of any good or service would be factored into it. This can be summarised as produc-ing 'more and more use values with less and less of nature. The law of economy of nature.'[37] Jason Hickel calls this 'radical abundance', the providing of universal public goods instead of relying on independent wealth to buy what people need. Public goods are about redistribution of social use towards the general population, away from the logic of individual consumer spending power.

Because the scope of human imagination and creativity is crushed by the death cult of capitalism, because the tyranny of capital is a form of psychic mutilation, we cannot under-estimate the role of desire, and the way that exceptional dynamism can be unleashed in a society free from exploitation and superfluous work. There is a desire to overcome limitations of capital and the social division of labour, leading to the immense release of human abilities once we have overcome them.

Kate Soper's work on an alternative hedonism is a useful way to challenge the argument that post-capitalism means austere living, a kind of 'hair-shirt future'. Soper imagines a future which is post-consumerist but hedonistic, finding pleasures beyond the limited horizons of owning consumer goods; 'the enjoyment that comes with having more time, doing more things for oneself, traveling more slowly and consuming less stuff'.[38] She challenges the techno-determinist views of some of the left, labelling them anti-humanist, too focused on robotics and with conventional views on consumption. But she is also opposed to the ascetic environmentalists who see only frugality. This is a radical vision of prosperity that breaks away from the ingrained capitalist view that progress and development is associated with economic growth: 'The demand for universal satisfaction of basic human needs must, therefore, be linked to a critique of the conception of human flourishing that has been promoted through the neo-liberal market, and needs now itself to be re-thought in the light of its deleterious consequences.'[39]

A focus on universal public services (or the social wage) instead of the relentless drive for capital accumulation and more money earned through selling commodities (including our own labour power) shifts the dynamic away from the individual to the social and creates space for a radical reconceptualisation of economic processes.

Conclusion

In 1992 the Union of Concerned Scientists wrote a public appeal about global warming: 'A great change in our stewardship of the Earth and the life on it is required if vast human misery is to be avoided and our global home on this planet is not to be irretrievably mutilated.' This new stewardship is a radical revolutionary new approach to organising human society. Nothing less will do. Some people might say that the description of a future world is just a fantasy, but the fundamental point for socialists is that we already have a society which can produce for our needs, and it is held back by private property, the marketplace and the profit motive. We can already have the good life if only we reorganise our society differently. We have made such revolutionary changes before. We will make them again. In fact, we have to make them again.

This book has outlined how we can eradicate the law of value that dominates our lives and create the basis for the meaning of work and human society to fundamentally change. We can build a society with a system of planned use-value production, where the social surplus is distributed and invested according to a democratically agreed plan. This will be carried out through participatory democratic institutions and coordination. It will be a global society where we live in a free association of equal producers and consumers. We can democratically decide how to use our remaining resources, how to balance production with sustainable growth, how to decarbonise and how to use new technologies that make life easier and more enjoyable.

It will not be a perfect society; there will still be choices to make over the direction society will go in, how we can improve life for everyone and how we can heal the metabolic rift properly, but it will be a society planned and organised by the great majority, free from the domination of capital and its inexorable relentless need to accumulate and destroy in order to create profit. We can finally have a rational economy, which means a society based on human values not shareholder bottom lines.

Everything that has been described in this book – a democratic social plan, workers' control, socialisation of production, cooperatives, trade unions, socialism itself – are all just concepts and tools that we can use to end the exploitation of class and the social oppression which is the legacy of human society so far. Socialism is the struggle to get there, where working people have the power, but they have not yet created the basis for society to evolve beyond commodity production towards a society based on human need. Even the future classless society of communism is only really a platform to get to where we need to go, as Marx argued: '*Communism* is the necessary form and the dynamic principle of the immediate future, but communism as such is not the goal of human development, the form of human society.'[1]

What are the political implications of the ideas in this book? First, that we have to get better at advocating a future world, at articulating what it might be like. We cannot just wage defensive struggles in the present or we will always be on the back foot, always fighting to stem the tide of reaction. It means mass education in political economy and socialism, ideas need to circulate, to breathe, to reach the minds of millions. It means being clear that we can fight against social oppression now but, until we get rid of capitalism and the class hierarchies that come with it, our battles against racism or sexism or queerphobia will only win limited gains. We have to a wage a relentless fight against the regressive idea that working-class people are all thick racists who hate the opera. Most of us are working people; we become a class when we fight collectively for our interests and against our exploiters and oppressors – and anything that undermines that united fight, whether it is nationalism or racism, is an enemy of the future.

It means a socialism starting from human liberation and environmental sustainability, no more pretending that authoritarian states masquerading as 'communist' are the future. We have to be able to raise anti-capitalist slogans and demands that go beyond 'tax the rich'. It isn't just about wealth redistribution but about control and power over our own lives. That isn't to say that demands around redistribution of wealth don't have a place, but unless we grasp the specific economics of capitalism and how it works to find ways to overthrow it then we will only ever be tinkering with a system that will ultimately ruin life on this planet and always restrict our lives to what profit requires or allows.

This means we cannot just fight for higher wages; we need to explain why we are even forced to rely on wages, and why we have so little control over how they are set. Anything which educates people in their exploitation is valid. It means organised work in trade unions and local communities to popularise the basic ideas of socialism, engaging in every struggle, making the links with an anti-capitalist perspective. The spirit dies without the struggle of the flesh, and history is decided by those people who take to the streets and fight for what they believe in. It also means a fight for radical empathy – unless we can find solidarity, and seek common cause, with humans across the world, we will be forever trapped in the dead end of racism or nationalism. It was noted by the US Army psychologist Captain G.M. Gilbert, at the Nuremberg Trials of leading Nazis after the Second World War, that what united all of them was the complete lack of empathy for others:

> In my work with the defendants, I was searching for the nature of evil and I now think I have come close to defining it. A lack of empathy. It's the one characteristic that connects all the defendants, a genuine incapacity to feel with their fellow men. Evil, I think, is the absence of empathy.[2]

That lack of empathy runs deep in the modern world, fostered by prejudice and hate to divide us from our common humanity.

This is what we should end with. This entire book has been about how post-capitalism could work, how we might end economic exploitation and social oppression. It ends on the possibility of a classless and stateless society in which we have genuine sustainability in a world of human freedom. But that will not be the end of our story. It will only be the beginning of a whole new world, a new way of being that will allow us to be truly ourselves, really free to explore our potential to the highest level. That future is something that we cannot even really begin to fathom, we are too weighed down by the misery and alienation of the present. But it is a future worth believing in and worth fighting for. Those fighting for a new world are like Monarch butterflies on their yearly migration from Canada to Mexico. It takes them four generations. Butterflies are born and die, never knowing their destination. Each contributes to the goal, helps the struggle to get closer. Who knows what generation we are? We know others came before and took us some of the way. Mistakes were made and lessons learned. But we are compelled by the disaster of the present to press ahead to something better.

I do not know what state the world will be in by the time you are reading this book, what conditions you will be fighting in or what changes can be won. But the lesson of history is that nothing remains the same and that the masses, inspired by hope for a better world, can achieve incredible things. Remember that.

Notes

Introduction

1. ICIJ, 'Offshore havens and hidden riches of world leaders and billionaires exposed in unprecedented leak', International Consortium of Investigative Journalists, 3 Oct. 2021 ($11.3 trillion was the number revealed by the Panama Papers).

2. 'Arctic nations are squaring up to exploit the region's rich natural resources', *Geographical*, 12 Aug. 2022.

3. 'Greenland startup begins shipping glacier ice to cocktail bars in the UAE', *Guardian*, 9 Jan. 2024.

4. Geoffrey Supran and Naomi Oreskes, 'Assessing ExxonMobil's climate change communications (1977–2014)', *Environmental Research Letters*, vol. 12, no. 8, https://iopscience.iop.org/article/10.1088/1748-9326/aa815f

5. 'Large rise in men referred to Prevent over women-hating incel ideology', *Guardian*, 26 Jan. 2023.

6. David Graeber, 'Revolution in reverse', *Radical Anthropology*, 1 (Oct. 2007), p. 8.

7. Rosa Luxemburg, *Reform and Revolution* (Dover Publications, 2012).

8. For an interesting discussion on the origin of this well-known phrase by Luxemburg see: 'The origin of Rosa Luxemburg's slogan "socialism or barbarism"', 22 Oct. 2014, https://climateandcapitalism.com/2014/10/22/origin-rosa-luxemburgs-slogan-socialism-barbarism/

9. As Cockshott and Cottrell argued in 1993, 'socialism will never again have any credibility as an economic system unless we can spell out [its] principles in reasonable detail'. W. Paul Cockshott and Allin Cottrell, *Towards a New Socialism* (Spokesman Books, 1993), p. 7.

10. István Mészáros, *Beyond Capital: Toward a Theory of Transition* (New York University Press, 1995), p. 729.

11. Sam Girdin, 'Socialism for realists', *Catalyst Journal*, 2018.

12. Karl Korsch cautioned that political economy under capital-
    ism means 'dealing with the material foundation of the existing
    bourgeois State' so 'for the proletariat first and foremost
    an enemy country'. Here we refer to a new kind of political
    economy based on the socialisation of the economy and its
    control through democratic decision making. See: Karl Korsch,
    Karl Marx (Russell & Russell, 1963).

13. Almost every socialist book on climate change contains at least
    an outline of the principles of a post-capitalist society now:
    Aaron Vansintjan, Andrea Vetter and Matthias Schmelzer, *The
    Future is Degrowth: A Guide to a World Beyond Capitalism* (Verso,
    2022); Martin Empson, *Socialism or Extinction: The Meaning
    of Revolution in a time of Ecological Crisis* (Bookmarks, 2022);
    Kate Soper, *Post-growth Living: For an Alternative Hedonism*
    (Verso, 2022); Kohei Saito, *Marx in the Anthropocene: Towards
    the Idea of Degrowth Communism* (Cambridge University Press,
    2023).

14. Troy Vettese and Drew Pendergrass, *Half-Earth Socialism: A
    Plan to Save the Future from Extinction, Climate Change and
    Pandemics* (Verso, 2022); M.E. O'Brien and Eman Abdel-
    hadi, *Everything for Everyone: An Oral History of the New York
    Commune, 2052–2072* (Common Notions Press, 2022).

15. Martin Empson, *Socialism or Extinction: The Meaning of Revo-
    lution in a time of Ecological Crisis* (Bookmarks, 2022) and Ted
    Reese, *Socialism or Extinction: Climate, Automation and War in
    the Final Capitalist Breakdown* (Self-published, 2020).

16. Jason Hickel, *Less is More* (Penguin, 2022).

17. Andy Hines blog at www.imaginingaftercapitalism.com

18. This idea that technology will automatically lead to communism
    is advocated by Ray Kurzweil, 'Technology will achieve the
    goals of communism' (online video, 2012), www.dailymotion.
    com/video/xm7xnn. For more see chapter 5.

19. Ronald Fraser, *Blood of Spain* (Pimlico, 1994), p. 137.

20. Marx's concern over the impact of capitalism on the environ-
    ment can be seen in *Capital*, vol. 1: 'All progress in capitalist
    agriculture is a progress in the art, not only of robbing the
    worker, but of robbing the soil…. Capitalist production,

therefore, only develops the techniques and the degree of combination of the social process of production by simultaneously undermining the original sources of all wealth – the soil and the worker.' The idea of the 'metabolic rift' was developed by John Bellamy Foster and Paul Burkett in *Monthly Review* based on their reading of Marx's writings. See John Bellamy Foster, 'Marx's theory of metabolic rift: Classical foundations for environmental sociology', *American Journal of Sociology*, vol. 105, no. 2 (Sept. 1999).

1   How Does Capitalism Work?

1. A good book on the theory of history is Jairus Banaji's *Theory as History* (Brill, 2010), which outlines that we shouldn't have a mechanical or deterministic view of history, but see historical laws abstract but as materially determined.

2. E.P. Thompson, 'The peculiarities of the English', *Socialist Register*, vol. 2 (1965), www.marxists.org/archive/thompson-ep/1965/english.htm

3. Perry Anderson, 'Theses on English class society', *International*, vol. 5, issue 1 (1979), pp. 16–17.

4. István Mészáros makes the distinction between capital and capitalism in *Beyond Capital*.

5. Reducing social relations to things (like money or commodities) is called 'reification'. See pp. 35 this volume.

6. For example, during the Covid-19 pandemic governments claimed to be following the science when it came to public health, but it was the requirements of capital as an economic logic that ultimately triumphed.

7. Benedict Anderson, *Imagined Communities Reflections on the Origin and Spread of Nationalism* (Verso, 2006).

8. Victor Wallis, *Socialist Practice: Histories and Theories* (Palgrave Macmillan, 2020), p. 83.

9. Larry Summers and others argued that this memo was meant to be sarcastic, though Summers later claimed that it was intended to provoke debate and he just hadn't read it very closely. Either way the memo isn't wrong about the economic logic.

10. 'Pollution and the poor', *The Economist*, 15 Feb. 1992.
11. Karl Marx and Frederick Engels, *The Communist Manifesto* (Verso, 2012).
12. Mészáros, *Beyond Capital*, p. 94.
13. See: 'NEWS: Sanders introduces legislation to enact a 32-hour workweek with no loss in pay', press release, 13 March 2024; Paul LaFargue, *The Right to be Lazy* (first published 1883), p. 30, www.marxists.org/archive/lafargue/1883/lazy/; Bregman, *Utopia for Realists*.
14. Mészáros, *Beyond Capital*.
15. Murray Smith, *Invisible Leviathan: Marx's Law of Value in the Twilight of Capitalism* (Brill, 2019), p. 318.
16. Ibid., p. 316.
17. This is a crucial difference between how the term 'exploitation' is traditionally used to mean unfair work or underpaid work, and what socialists mean by it which is simply all waged labour.
18. See U.S. Bureau of Labor Statistics, 'Entrepreneurship and the U.S. economy', www.bls.gov/bdm/entrepreneurship/entrepreneurship.htm
19. 'By striving to reduce labour time to a minimum, while, on the other hand, positing labour time as the sole measure and source of wealth, capital itself is a contradiction-in-progress.' Karl Marx, *Outlines of the Critique of Political Economy* (Rough draft of 1857–58), in Marx and Engels, *Collected Works*, vol. 28 (International Publishers, 1987), p. 91.
20. 'What determines value is not the time taken to produce a thing, but the *minimum* time it could possibly be produced in, and this minimum is ascertained by competition.' Karl Marx, *The Poverty of Philosophy*, in Marx and Engels, *Collected Works*, vol. 6 (International Publishers, 1976), p. 136.
21. 'Europe's hidden milk lake threatens fragile market', *Politico*, Jan. 2018, www.politico.eu/article/europes-hidden-milk-price-lake-threatens-fragile-market-eu-commission/
22. *Inside Edition*, 'Ohio pizzeria owner gives staff entire day's profits, each getting $78 per hour, on Employee Appreciation Day', 14 July 2021.
23. This is Marx's specific contribution to the labour theory of value. David Ricardo understood it only as concrete labour,

a specific worker doing a specific piece of work and creating surplus value because they were not paid the value of what they produced. Marx introduced the idea that actually the social surplus is decided by the massed abstract labour of workers, the socially necessary labour time that is abstract labour across the entire economy.

24. Karl Marx, *Capital*, vol. 1 (Lawrence & Wishart, 1977), p. 46.

25. 'Capital in general, as distinct from the particular capitals, does indeed appear only as an abstraction; not an arbitrary abstraction, but an abstraction which grasps the specific characteristics which distinguish capital from all other forms of wealth.' Marx, *Grundrisse* (Penguin, 1973), p. 449.

26. Nicholas Vrousalis, 'Capital without wage-labour: Marx's mode of subsumption revisited', *Economics and Philosophy*, vol. 34 (2018), p. 413.

27. 'Only as an inner law, vis-à-vis the individual agents, as a blind law of nature, does the law of value exert its influence here and maintain the social equilibrium of production amidst its accidental fluctuations.' Marx, *Capital*, vol. 3 (Lawrence & Wishart, 1975), p. 880.

28. Ernest Mandel, *Key Problems in the Transition from Capitalism to Socialism* (Merit, 1969), p. 41.

29. I.I. Rubin, *Essays on Marx's Theory of Value* (Pattern Books, 2020), p. 152.

30. Marx, *The Poverty of Philosophy* in Marx and Engels, *Collected Works*, vol. 6, pp. 41–2.

31. For instance see Juliet B. Schor, *The Overworked American: The Unexpected Decline of Leisure* (Basic Books, 1992).

32. Marx, *Grundrisse*, p. 145.

33. Marx, *The Poverty of Philosophy* (Cosimo, 2008), p. 87.

34. Marx, *Capital*, vol. 1, pp. 76–87.

35. Val Burris, 'Reification: A Marxist perspective', *California Sociologist*, vol. 10, no. 1 (1988).

36. Michael A. Lebowitz, *The Socialist Imperative: From Gotha to Now* (Monthly Review Press, 2015), p. 8.

37. Karl Marx and Frederick Engels, *The German Ideology* (Lawrence & Wishart, 1970), p. 64.

38. *Outlines of the Critique of Political Economy* (Rough draft of 1857–58), in Marx and Engels *Collected Works*, vol. 28, p. 389. Also read Peter Hudis, *Marx's Alternatives to Capitalism* (Brill, 2012), pp. 155–6.

39. Simon Sutterlütti and Stefan Meretz, *Make Capitalism History: A Practical Framework for Utopia and the Transformation of Society* (Palgrave Macmillan, 2023), p. 76.

40. István Mészáros, *Social Structure and Forms of Consciousness*, vol. 2 (Monthly Review, 2012): 'capital always is – and, this cannot be stressed strongly enough, it always must remain, as a matter of inner systemic determination – insuperably scarce, even when under certain conditions it is contradictorily over-produced', p. 304.

41. Hickel, *Less is More*.

42. Smith, *Invisible Leviathan*, pp. 323–4.

43. Hickel, *Less is More*: 'creates needs for anti-depressants, sleep aids, alcohol, dieticians, marital counselling, expensive holidays, and other products people would otherwise be less likely to require'.

44. Bertell Ollman, 'Marx's vision of communism: A reconstruction', *Critique*, vol. 8, no. 1 (1977), p. 27.

45. 'Mayor of London says economic inequality can be good, and some people are just too dumb to succeed', *Business Insider*, 28 Nov. 2013.

46. Paul S. Adler, *The 99 percent Econ%my: How Democratic Socialism Can Overcome the Crises of Capitalism* (Oxford University Press, 2019), p. 27.

47. Marx and Engels, *Communist Manifesto*.

48. 'Pre-capitalist crisis is a crisis of under-production of use-values…. A capitalist crisis, however, is a crisis of over-production of exchange-values', Ernest Mandel, *Marxist Economic Theory*, vol. 1 (Merlin, 1977), p. 343.

49. Marx, in *Theories of Surplus Value*, vol. 2 (Lawrence & Wishart, 1969). Andrew Kliman talks more about this in *The Failure of Capitalist Production: Underlying Causes of the Great Recession* (London: Pluto Press, 2011).

50. Hadas Thier, *A People's Guide to Capitalism* (Haymarket Books, 2020), p. 154.

51. Joan Robinson, quoted in Erik Olin Wright, *Envisioning Utopias* (Verso, 2010), p. 200.

52. Giovanni Arrighi, 'Financial expansions in world historical perspective: A reply to Robert Pollin', *New Left Review*, July/Aug. 1997.

53. The Marxist economist Henryk Grossman argued in the 1920s that capitalist over-accumulation would tend towards a point of zero profit and zero GDP, a final breakdown moment. Ted Reese updates this argument in *Socialism or Extinction*.

54. Smith, *Invisible Leviathan*, p. 328.

55. Marx: 'Humans live from nature, i.e.: nature is our body, and we must maintain a continuing dialogue with it if we are not to die. To say that humanity's physical and mental life is linked to nature simply means that nature is linked to itself, for humans are part of nature.' Marx and Engels *Collected Works*, vol. 3 (Lawrence & Wishart, 1975), p. 276.

56. Marx, *Capital*, vol. 1, p. 50: 'So far therefore as labour is a creator of use value, is useful labour, it is a necessary condition, independent of all forms of society, for the existence of the human race; it is an eternal nature-imposed necessity, without which there can be no material exchanges between man and Nature, and therefore no life.' Anyone arguing for a complete retreat of humanity from nature is arguing for an impossibility.

57. For a breakdown of the factors into pricing a bottle of water see https://drinkflowater.com/the-real-cost-of-bottled-water-2/ – notably it is 20 per cent for sales and marketing, production is 10 per cent. The cost of the water is functionally zero but three times as much water is used to make one bottle. A literal waste.

58. 'an irreparable rift in the interdependent process of the social metabolism, a metabolism prescribed by the natural laws of life itself'. Bellamy Foster, 'Marx's theory of metabolic rift'.

59. Kohei Saito, *Marx in the Anthropocene: Towards the Idea of Degrowth Communism* (Cambridge University Press, 2023).

60. The Salvage Collective, *The Tragedy of the Worker: Towards the Proletarocene* (Verso, 2021), p. 2.

61. Cited in Paul Murphy, 'Quarter-Earth reformism' (review of Paul Huber's *Climate Change as Class War*), *Rupture*, 10 April 2023.

62. Saito, *Marx in the Anthropocene*, pp. 29–34.
63. Andreas Malm, *Fossil Capital: The Rise of Steam Power and the Roots of Global Warming* (Verso, 2016).
64. Salvage Collective, *The Tragedy of the Worker*.
65. 'Big Oil doubles profits in blockbuster 2022', *Reuters*, 8 Feb. 2023.
66. V.I. Lenin, *Imperialism: The Highest Age of Capitalism*, in Lenin, *Selected Works* (Foreign Languages Publishing House, 1952).
67. Saito, *Marx in the Anthropocene*, p. 2.
68. John Bellamy Foster, John Molyneux and Owen McCormack, 'Against Doomsday scenarios: What is to be done now?', *Monthly Review*, 1 Dec. 2021.
69. Jason Hickel et al., 'Imperialist appropriation in the world economy: Drain from the global South through unequal exchange 1990–2015', *Global Environmental Change*, vol. 73 (March 2022).
70. See Utsa Patnaik and Prabhat Patnaik, *Capital and Imperialism: Theory, History, and the Present* (Monthly Review, 2021).
71. Gurminder K. Bhambra, 'Relations of extraction, relations of redistribution: Empire, nation, and the construction of the British welfare state', *British Journal of Sociology*, vol. 73, no. 1 (Jan. 2022).
72. 'None of this is to say that workers in the core are not exploited; it is merely to point out that they benefit from a capitalist system that pits them against their peripheral counterparts. If you drink coffee in the United States or Europe, eat chocolate, own a phone or wear clothes, you are in all likelihood a participant in the super-exploitation of the periphery's lands and labour. To recognise this is a precondition for meaningful internationalism.' Kai Heron, 'The Great Unfettering', *New Left Review*, 7 Sept. 2022.
73. William I. Robinson, 'The unbearable Manicheanism of the "anti-imperialist" left', *The Philosophical Salon*, 7 Aug. 2023.
74. Wallis, *Socialist Practice*, p. xii.
75. W. Paul Cockshott and Allin Cottrell, 'Reflections on economic democracy', in Paul Zarembka (ed.), *The Capitalist State and Its Economy: Democracy in Socialism* (Emerald Publishing, 2005), p. 222.

76. Peter Hudis argues that: 'The joint-stock company can in no way be considered an expression of "socialism". At the same time, the joint-stock company represents a possible *transitional* form *towards* a new social order, in that it undermines the principle of private ownership of the means of production. In doing so, it helps prepare the ground for a form of socialisation that can overcome the separation of the labourers from the conditions of production.' Hudis, *Marx's Alternatives*, p. 177.

77. 'US military consumes more hydrocarbons than most countries – with a massive hidden impact on the climate', Lancaster University, 20 June 2019, www.lancaster.ac.uk/news/us-military-consumes-more-hydrocarbons-than-most-countries-with-a-massive-hidden-impact-on-the-climate

2   A Living Movement for Socialism

1. Marx, *The Civil War in France* (Foreign Languages Press, 1970).
2. V. I. Lenin, 'The collapse of the Second International', in Lenin, *Collected Works*, vol. 21 (Progress Publishers, 1974).
3. Marx, *Grundrisse*, p. 227.
4. Mészáros, *Beyond Capital*, p. 425.
5. Asef Bayat, 'Workers' control after the revolution', *Middle East Research and Information Project*, issue 113 (March/April 1983).
6. Michael Szporer, 'Anna Walentynowicz and the legacy of Solidarity in Poland', *Journal of Cold War Studies*, vol. 13, no. 1 (2011).
7. Empresas recuperadas por sus trabajadores, or ERTs. See: www.workerscontrol.net/authors/crisis-capitalism-argentina%E2%80%99s-worker-recuperated-enterprises-and-possibilities-another-world
8. Donald Reid, *Opening the Gates: The Lip Affair, 1968–1981* (Verso, 2018).
9. Kiraz Janicke, 'Venezuela's co-managed Inveval: Surviving in a sea of capitalism', *Venezuela Analysis*, 27 July 2007.
10. Hilary Wainwright and Dave Elliot, *The Lucas Plan: A New Trade Unionism in the Making?* (Spokesman Books, 2018).

11. Yousaf Nishat-Botero, 'Planning's ecologies: Democratic planning in the age of planetary crises', *Organization*, June 2023.

12. Teresa R. Melgar, *A Time of Closure? Participatory Budgeting in Porto Alegre, Brazil, after the Workers' Party Era* (Cambridge University Press: 2014).

13. Alice Martin and Annie Quick, *Unions Renewed: Building Power in an Age of Finance* (Polity Press, 2020).

14. Michael Löwy, *Ecosocialism* (Haymarket, 2015), p. 31.

15. Karl Marx, *Conspectus of Bakunin's Statism and Anarchy* (1874), www.marxists.org/archive/marx/works/1874/04/bakun-in-notes.htm

16. For more on this see Brett Christophers, *Rentier Capitalism: Who Owns the Economy, and Who Pays for It?* (Verso, 2020).

17. This is one of the main disagreements between Marxists and anarchists. Anarchists generally are more optimistic that workers can generate revolutionary politics in a given situation and criticise Marxists, and especially Leninists, for not having faith in the people to develop their own strategy.

18. Frederick Douglass, 'If there is no struggle, there is no progress', 3 Aug. 1857, www.blackpast.org/african-american-history/1857-frederick-douglass-if-there-no-struggle-there-no-progress/

19. Leon Trotsky, *The Transitional Programme for Socialist Revolution* (Pathfinder Press, 1977).

20. Cockshott and Cottrell, 'Reflections on *Towards a New Socialism*', 3rd draft of new Preface to *Towards a New Socialism*, p. 223, www.academia.edu/1119122/Towards_a_New_Socialism_New_preface_3rd_draft

21. Leon Trotsky, *The Transitional Programme for Socialist Revolution*.

22. Ibid.

23. John Holloway, *Change the World without Taking Power* (Pluto, 2002).

3   The Post-capitalist Society

1. In debates in the early days of the Soviet Union, Nikolai Bukharin argued that the law of value was a kind of tran-

shistorical economic law, but this is a minority view within Marxist economics.

2. These three requirements are how Pat Devine summarises a transitional society. Pat Devine, *Democracy and Economic Planning: The Political Economy of a Self-governing Society* (Polity, 1989), p. 113. I have added the fourth on commodity production.

3. Kamal Khosravi, 'Abstract labour and socialism', *Historical Materialism*, vol. 34, no. 4 (2023): 236–60.

4. Simon Hannah, 'Democracy is key to tackling environmental degradation', 21 July 2023, https://anticapitalistresistance.org/democracy-is-key-to-tackling-environmental-degradation/.

5. Leon Trotsky, 'The Soviet economy in danger: Conditions and methods of planned economy', www.marxists.org/archive/trotsky/1932/10/sovecon.htm

6. Aaron Benanav, 'Socialist investment, dynamic planning, and the politics of human need', *Rethinking Marxism*, vol. 34, no. 2 (2022), p. 197.

7. Löwy, *Ecosocialism*, p. 299.

8. Saito, *Marx in the Anthropocene*, pp. 241–3.

9. Cédric Durand, Elena Hofferberth and Matthias Schmelzer, 'Planning beyond growth: The case for economic democracy within ecological limits', *Journal of Cleaner Production*, vol. 437 (January 2024), p. 15.

10. Ernest Mandel, 'In defense of socialist planning', *New Left Review*, 159 (Sept.–Oct. 1986).

11. Devine, *Democracy and Economic Planning*.

12. Richard Schmitt, 'Socialist democracy and solidarity', *Socialism and Democracy*, vol. 39, issue 1 (2015), p. 67.

13. *Ludwig Feuerbach, Karl Marx, Friedrich Engels: German Socialist Philosophy* (Continuum, 1997), p. 239.

14. Devine, *Democracy and Economic Planning*, argues for an idea of a civil society under socialism and Benanav takes up this view in his writing in 'Socialist investment, dynamic planning, and the politics of human need'. The stronger arguments for post-capitalist society steer away from the idea of a single party that controls all aspects of political and social life, as happened in Russia and China.

15. For the Second World War as a comparison, see Paul S. Adler, 'Capitalism, socialism, and the climate crisis', *Organization Theory*, vol. 3, no. 1 (2022), for War Communism see Andreas Malm, *Corona, Climate, Chronic Emergency: War Communism in the Twenty-first Century* (Verso, 2022).

16. For more information see: https://ourworldindata.org/green house-gas-emissions

17. Löwy, *Ecosocialism*, pp. 297–8.

18. Andrew Simms, *21 Hours: Why a Shorter Working Week Can Help Us All to Flourish in the 21st Century* (NEF, 2010).

19. Paul Lafargue, *The Right to be Lazy* (Pattern Books, 2020).

20. David Graeber, *Bullshit Jobs* (Simon & Schuster, 2018).

21. Aaron Benanav, *Automation and the Future of Work* (Verso, 2020), p. 86.

22. Michael Albert: 'if you work at a particularly unpleasant and disempowering task for some time each day or week, then for some other time you should work at more pleasant and empowering tasks'. *Parecon: Life after Capitalism* (Verso, 2003), ch. 6. Available on Znetwork.org

23. Löwy, *Ecosocialism*, p. 26: 'It is important to emphasise, as well, that planning is not in contradiction with workers' self-management of their productive units. While the decision, made through the planning system, to transform, say, an auto-plant into one producing buses and trams would be taken by society as a whole, the internal organisation and functioning of the plant should be democratically managed by its own workers.'

24. 'If all that is required for socialism is production according to a plan, for use and not for profit, under the supervision of an authoritarian command structure, then the prison workshop is the proper prototype of a socialist community.' Walter Kendall, *State Ownership, Workers' Control and Socialism* (Square One Publications, 1972).

25. Wallis, *Socialist Practice*, p. 98.

26. Al Campbell, 'Democratic planned socialism: Feasible economic procedures', *Science & Society*, vol. 66, no. 1, special issue, *Building Socialism Theoretically: Alternatives to Capitalism and the Invisible Hand* (spring 2002), p. 33.

27. Ibid.

28. Smith, *Invisible Leviathan*, p. 319.

29. Karl Kautsky, *The Social Revolution and the Mirror of the Social Revolution*, vol. 2 (The Twentieth Century Press, 1903), p. 24. 'Trusts' here refers to the monopolies that emerge under capitalism.

30. Löwy, *Ecosocialism*.

31. Catherine Samary, *Plan, Markets and Democracy* (IIRE – International Institute for Research and Education, 1998), p. 7.

32. Ernest Germain (Mandel), 'The law of value in relation to self-management and investment in the economy of the workers' states', *World Outlook* [Paris], no .14 (1963), www.marxists.org/archive/mandel/1963/xx/value-self-man.html

33. Classical socialist economics makes a distinction between Department I (capital that makes capital) and Department II (consumer goods). Department I is the big machinery and plant that most of us never really come across, capable of producing the tools and machinery for Department II. Department II produces the things most of us use: shoes, food, books, computers and so on. Some had added a Department III, which covers insurance, media, advertising, etc. Expansion of Department I is not usually immediately noticed by most people, but it is essential to provide a firm industrial basis for future production. Lack of investment in this area leads to inefficient and wasteful production in Department II. Getting the balance right between these two parts of the economy will be a central task of any socialist democracy.

34. At a speech of the Manchester Branch of the First International in 1872, Marx described how: 'The nationalisation of land will work a complete change in the relations between labour and capital, and finally, do away with the capitalist form of production, whether industrial or rural. Then class distinctions and privileges will disappear together with the economical basis upon which they rest. To live on other people's labour will become a thing of the past. There will be no longer any government or state power, distinct from society itself! Agriculture, mining, manufacture, in one word, all branches of production, will gradually be organised in the most adequate

manner. National *centralisation of the means of production* will become the national basis of a society composed of associations of free and equal producers, carrying on the social business on a common and rational plan.' See: www.marxists.org/archive/marx/works/1872/04/nationalisation-land.htm

35. Marx and Engels, *Communist Manifesto*, p. 175.

36. Kautsky, *The Social Revolution*, vol. 2, p. 8.

37. Marx, *Grundrisse*, pp. 155–6.

38. 'The installation of a system of payment by labour tokens is incompatible with paying interest, since the money in which the interest payments were made will cease to be legal tender. By this point, the essentially parasitic nature of the rentier class will be generally evident, since they would have lost any remaining productive function.' Cockshott and Cottrell, 'Reflections on economic democracy', p. 235.

39. Rutger Bregman, *Utopia for Realists* (Bloomsbury, 2018), pp. 203–30.

40. Otto Neurath, *Empiricism and Sociology* (D. Reidel, 1973), p. 278.

41. Durand et al., 'Planning beyond growth', p. 11.

42. Jason Hickel, Daniel W. O'Neill, Andrew L. Fanning, and Huzaifa Zoomkawala, 2022. 'National responsibility for ecological breakdown: A fair-shares assessment of resource use, 1970–2017', *The Lancet: Planetary Health*, vol. 6, no. 4 (2022): e342–49.

43. Jason Hickel, 'Accelerationist possibilities in an ecosocialist degrowth scenario', blog, 21 Dec. 2023, www.jasonhickel.org/blog/2023/12/21/accelerationist-possibilities-in-an-ecosocialist-degrowth-scenario

44. A Pigouvian tax is a financial fee associated with harmful activity whereby the external consequences of producing or consuming something are recompensed. This was developed by English economist Arthur Cecil Pigou (1877–1959), who also came up with the concept of externalities.

45. Matt Huber, 'Mish-mash ecologism', *NLR – Sidecar*, 18 Aug. 2022, https://newleftreview.org/sidecar/posts/mish-mash-ecologism

46. As Huber points out, these developments are only 'techno-fixes' when they are proposed under existing capitalism since the entrenched interests of existing fossil capital resist them until it is too late, when there will be a rush to develop the technology needed.

47. Hickel, *Less is More*, p. 219.

48. For more on this see Jonathan Neale, *Fight the Fire* (Resistance Books, 2021).

49. W.P. Cockshott, A. Cottrell and J.P. Dapprich, *Economic Planning in an Age of Climate Crisis* (Self-published, 2022), pp. 61–2.

50. From Pete Seeger's 2008 album *At 89*, Appleseed Records.

51. Ollman, 'Marx's vision of communism: A reconstruction', p. 27.

52. Jason Hickel, 'From ownership to usership', in *Less is More*, p. 217. Sharing tools and other items with neighbours when not needed was regularly practised by some First Nations American tribes as Potlatch before Christian missionaries and state governors banned the practice.

53. Adler, 'Capitalism, socialism, and the climate crisis'.

54. Devine, *Democracy and Economic Planning*, pp. 129–30, proposes to collectivise small businesses and cooperatives when they grow to a certain point.

55. Jamie Merchant, 'Fantasies of secession: A critique of left economic nationalism', *The Brooklyn Rail*, Feb. 2018.

56. Karl Marx and Frederick Engels, *The German Ideology* (International Publishers, 1970), p. 55.

57. Matt Huber, *Climate Change as Class War: Building Socialism on a Warming Planet* (Verso, 2022). 'Land back' is a term used mainly in the US referring to the return of land to Indigenous people.

58. Andreas Malm, 'transactions that might seem fair on the monetary surface, but allow rich countries to absorb biophysical resources from the poor and drain their natural endowments.' *Corona, Climate, Chronic Emergency*, p. 52.

59. Wallis, *Socialist Practice*, p. xiii.

60. 'Money cannot be arbitrarily "abolished," nor the state and the old family "liquidated." They have to exhaust their historic mission, evaporate, and fall away. The deathblow to money

fetishism will be struck only upon that stage when the steady growth of social wealth has made us bipeds forget our miserly attitude toward every excess minute of labor, and our humiliating fear about the size of our ration. Having lost its ability to bring happiness or trample men in the dust, money will turn into mere bookkeeping receipts for the convenience of statisticians and for planning purposes. In the still more distant future, probably these receipts will not be needed. But we can leave this question entirely to posterity, who will be more intelligent than we are.' Leon Trotsky, *The Revolution Betrayed* (Dover Publications, 2004), p. 50.

61. V.I. Lenin, 'The deception of the people by the slogans of equality and freedom', in Little Lenin Library, vol. 19, pp. 26, 35–6.

62. 'Plan versus market', *Trotskyist Bulletin*, Oct. 1996, p. 35.

63. Mandel, *Marxist Economic Theory*, p. 659.

64. Saito, *Marx in the Anthropocene*, pp. 230–1.

65. 'For real wealth is the developed productive power of all individuals. The measure of wealth is then not any longer, in any way, labour time, but rather disposable time.' Marx, *Grundrisse*, p. 708.

66. Tithi Bhattacharya (ed.), *Social Reproduction Theory: Remapping Class, Recentering Oppression* (Pluto Press, 2017), p. 92.

67. Benanav, *Automation and the Future of Work*, p. 87.

68. James P. Cannon, *What Socialist America Will Look Like* (Resistance Books, 2001).

69. Dolores Hayden, *The Domestic Revolution* (MIT Press, 1981).

70. Serap Saritas Oran, in Bhattacharya (ed.) *Social Reproduction Theory*, p. 150: 'Pensions are associated with the socialised costs of the means of consumption of the nonworking members of the working-class.'

71. This mainly happened on Twitter, so make of that what you will.

72. 'Winston Churchill feared that the Ministry of Food's original moniker – 'communal feeding centres' – was too 'redolent of communism and the workhouse'. Dr Bryce Evans, 'National kitchens: Communal dining in wartime', *The Gazette*, www.thegazette.co.uk/all-notices/content/100292.

73. Ibid.
74. Lily Baun, *Frauenarbeit und Hauswirtschaft* (Women's work and housekeeping) (Buchhandlung Vorwärts, 1901).
75. For more on this read Jason Hickel, *Less is More*.
76. Nick Rogers, 'Reflections on the economics of socialism', *Journal of Global Faultlines*, vol. 9, no. 2, pp. 152–3.
77. Lenin, *Collected Works*, 2nd English edn, vol. 45 (Progress Publishers, 1976), pp. 601–2.
78. Leon Trotsky, *The Challenge of the Left Opposition (1926–1927)* (Pathfinder Press, 1980), p. 58.
79. Lenin, *Collected Works*, 2nd English edn, vol. 33 (Progress Publishers, 1965), pp. 455–9.
80. August Bebel, *Society of the Future* (Progress Publishers, 1976), p. 30.
81. John Stuart Mill, *Political Economy*, cited in Bebel, *Society of the Future*, p. 30 (footnote).
82. 'Thus, economy of time, along with the planned distribution of labour time among the various branches of production, remains the first economic law on the basis of communal production.' Marx, *Grundrisse*, p. 173.
83. 'Men are products of circumstances and upbringing and therefore changed men are products of other circumstances and changed upbringing.' Marx, *Theses on Feuerbach* (Progress Publishers, 1983).
84. Löwy, *Ecosocialism*, p. 304.
85. William Morris, 'Looking backward', *Commonweal*, vol. 5, no. 180 (June 1889), www.marxists.org/archive/morris/works/1889/commonweal/06-bellamy.htm
86. Aaron Jaffe, *Social Reproduction Theory and the Socialist Horizon: Work, Power and Political Strategy* (Pluto, 2020), p. 238.
87. 'When society is freed from the narrow drive to augment value as an end in itself, it can turn its attention to supplying the multiplicity of needs and wants that are integral to the social individual.' Peter Hudis, 'Yes, there is an alternative – and it can be found in Marx', International Marxist Humanist Organisation, 20 February 2015.
88. Smith, *Invisible Leviathan*, p. 54.

89. Ernest Mandel, 'In defence of socialist planning', *New Left Review*, no. 159 (Sept.–Oct. 1986), pp. 5–37.

90. In Boris Pasternak's anti-Bolshevik novel *Dr Zhivago*, the despotic policeman Strelnikov personifies the bureaucratic and cruel manners of the 'revolutionary' policeman: 'The personal life is dead in Russia. History has killed it.'

91. Mandel, 'In defence of socialist planning'.

92. Saito, *Marx in the Anthropocene*, p. 233.

93. Stephen Jay Gould, *The Panda's Thumb: More Reflections in Natural History* (W.W. Norton, 1980).

94. Mandel, 'In defence of socialist planning'.

95. Girdin, 'Socialism for realists'.

96. Marx, *The Civil War in France*.

97. Wassily Leontief, 'National economic planning: Methods and problems', *Challenge*, vol. 19, no. 3 (1976), p. 8.

98. Devine, *Democracy and Economic Planning*, p. 201 and pp. 270–2.

99. Frédéric Legault and Simon Tremblay-Pepin, *A Brief Sketch of Three Models of Democratic Economic Planning* (CRITS – Research Centre on Social Innovation and Transformation, April 2021), https://innovationsocialeusp.ca/wp-content/uploads/2021/04/Note-2-Legault-and-Tremblay-Pepin-Democratic-Planning.pdf

100. John Riddell, 'Socialist planning and the bureaucratic economy', 2015, https://johnriddell.com/2015/05/17/socialist-planning-and-the-bureaucratic-economy/

101. Benanav, 'Socialist investment, dynamic planning, and the politics of human need', p. 193.

102. Ibid., pp. 198–200.

103. Joel Kovel, *The Enemy of Nature: The End of Capitalism or the End of the World?* (Zed Books, 2007), p. 215.

104. Max Grunberg, 'The planning daemon: Future desire and communal production', *Historical Materialism*, 27 March 2023.

105. Marx, *Capital*, vol. 2, p. 199.

106. Marx and Engels state, in *The German Ideology*, that 'the production, as well as the satisfaction … of needs is a historical process, which is not found in the case of a sheep or dog'.

107. Aaron Bastani, *Fully Automated Luxury Capitalism* (Verso, 2019).

108. Saito, *Marx in the Anthropocene*, p. 222.

109. Stephen Ward (ed.), *Pages from a Black Radical's Notebook: A James Boggs Reader* (Wayne State University Press, 2011), p. 219.

110. Rep. Thaddeus McCotter said in his speech to Congress: 'In the Bolshevik Revolution, the slogan was "Peace, land, and bread,"' McCotter said: 'Today, you are being made to choose between bread and freedom. I suggest the people on Main Street have said they prefer their freedom, and I am with them.'

111. When the masses took control of Paris in 1871 and replaced the city government with a very simple commune structure, Marx heralded it as a huge step forward: 'It was a Revolution against the *State* itself, this supernaturalist abortion of society, a resumption by the people for the people, of its own social life. It was not a revolution to transfer it from one fraction of the ruling classes to the other, but a Revolution to break down this horrid machinery of class domination itself.' 'Drafts of *The Civil War in France*', in *Marx and Engels Collected Works*, vol. 22 (International Publishers, 1986).

112. Friedrich Engels, *Socialism: Utopian and Scientific* (Charles H. Kerr, 1908), pp. 128–9).

113. 'When in the course of development, class distinctions have disappeared and all production has been concentrated in the hands of a vast association of the whole nation, the public power will lose its political character. Political power, properly so called, is merely the organised power of one class for the oppressing of another.' Marx and Engels, *The Communist Manifesto*, in Karl Marx, *Selected Writings* (Hackett Publishing, 1994), p. 176.

114. Frederick Engels, *Herr Eugen Dühring's Revolution in Science* [Anti-Dühring] (Lawrence & Wishart, 1961), p. 311.

115. Karl Marx, Preface to *A Contribution to the Critique of Political Economy* (1859).

116. Nikolai Bukharin and Evgenii Preobrezhensky, *The ABC of Communism*, first published in English in 1922, www.marxists. org/archive/bukharin/works/1920/abc/index.htm

117. Adam Schaff, *Marxism and the Human Individual* (McGraw-Hill, 1970), p. 181.

4 Arguments against Socialism: Human Nature and Knowledge

1. *Sunday Times*, 3 May 1981.
2. W. Arthur Lewis, *The Principles of Economic Planning* (Psychology Press, 2003), pp. 7–8.
3. Marx, *Poverty of Philosophy*.
4. Marx, *The German Ideology*.
5. Allman writes from an educational theorist's perspective. In particular read Paula Allman, *On Marx: An Introduction to the Revolutionary Intellect of Karl Marx* (Brill, 2007).
6. Hegel's *Philosophy of History*, III. *Philosophic History* (Dover Publications, 2012), p. 21.
7. Leszek Kolakowski, *Main Currents of Marxism*, vol. 1: *The Founders* (Clarendon Press, 1978), p. 138.
8. Allman, *On Marx*, pp. 33–4.
9. Ibid., p. 34.
10. Allin Cottrell and W. Paul Cockshott, 'Calculation, complexity and planning: The socialist calculation debate once again', *Review of Political Economy*, vol. 5, no. 1 (July 1993), p. 78.
11. Ludwig von Mises, *Economic Calculation in the Socialist Commonwealth* (George Routledge & Sons, 1935).
12. Ibid.
13. Ludwig von Mises, *Collectivist Economic Planning*, edited by F.A. Hayek (Routledge & Kegan Paul, 1935), p. 104.
14. F.A. Hayek, 'The use of knowledge in society', *American Economic Review*, vol. 35, no. 4 (Sept. 1945), pp. 519–20.
15. Joseph Stiglitz, *Whither Socialism?* (MIT Press, 1994), p. 9.
16. John O'Neill, 'Socialism, associations and the market', *Economy and Society*, vol. 32, no. 2 (2003), pp. 184–5.
17. Richard Day, 'Introduction' in P. Maksakovsky, *The Capitalist Cycle* (Haymarket, 2009), p. xlii.
18. For instance, see *A Beginner's Guide to Central Planning*, 16 Sept. 2014, https://humanprogress.org/a-beginners-guide-to-socialist-economics/

19. Summarised by Fred Magdoff and Chris Williams in 'Capitalist economies create waste', *truthout*, 17 Aug. 2017.

20. 'Globally, around 14 percent of food produced is lost between harvest and retail, while an estimated 17 percent of total global food production is wasted (11 percent in households, 5 percent in the food service and 2 percent in retail).' www.un.org/en/observances/end-food-waste-day

21. Adler, 'Capitalism, socialism, and the climate crisis'.

22. For instance, Joseph Schumpeter argues that innovations come from individual entrepreneurs, a core idea that intersects the power of the individual with the structure of the market – perfect for legitimising capitalism.

23. For instance see Andrea Laplane and Mariana Mazzucato, 'Socialising the risks and rewards of public investments: Economic, policy and legal issues', Working Paper, UCL 2019–09.

24. 'State of innovation: Busting the private-sector myth', *New Scientist*, 21 Aug. 2013.

25. Ibid.

26. Recent examples include the Gulf Railway Line, over budget by up to \$11 billion; Berlin Brandenburg Airport; HS2 railway in the UK, over budget by £66 billion; expansion of the New York Metro from Long Island to Grand Central Station; the Big Dig in Boston, over budget by \$12 billion; Crossrail in London, £3 billion over budget; Navi Mumbai International Airport, India, over budget by \$1.5 billion; Stuttgart 21 rail, over budget by \$6.8 billion; California high-speed rail, a massive \$72bn over budget. The list goes on.

27. Engels, 'Speech in Elberfeld 1845', in Marx and Engels, *Collected Works*, vol. 4, p. 243.

28. Ibid.

29. Mandel, 'In defence of socialist planning'.

30. Ibid.

31. V.I. Lenin, 'The party crisis', 19 Jan. 1921, in *Collected Works*, vol. 32 (Progress Publishers, 1965).

32. Lenin, 'Speech on the anniversary of the revolution', at the Extraordinary Sixth All-Russia Congress of Soviets of

Workers', Peasants', Cossacks' and Red Army Deputies, 6 Nov. 1918.

33. Cockshott and Cottrell, *Towards a New Socialism*, p. 5.

34. Mandel, *Marxist Economic Theory*, p. 655.

35. 'Two workers who were employed to unload bricks quickly from trucks did so by throwing them on the ground, usually breaking 30 per cent of them.' Quoted in Moshe Lewin's *Stalinism and the Seeds of Soviet Reform* (London: Pluto Press, 1991), p. 148.

36. Frank Furedi, *The Soviet Union Demystified* (Junius, 1986), p. 149.

37. H.H. Ticktin, 'Towards a political economy of the USSR', *Critique*, vol. 1, issue 1 (spring 1973), p. 25.

38. Ernest Mandel, 'Economics of the transition period', in *50 Years of World Revolution – An International Symposium* (Merit, 1968), p. 285.

39. Michael Ellman, *Socialist Planning* (Cambridge University Press, 2014), p. 12.

40. Michael Löwy points to the difference between socialism and the Stalinist system: 'the aim of socialism is not to produce more and more commodities, but to give human beings free time to fully develop their potentialities. To this extent they have little in common with "productivism", i.e. with the idea that the unlimited expansion of production is an aim in itself.' 'Ecosocialism and democratic planning', *Socialist Review* (2007) p. 295.

41. Brian Green, *Planning the Future* (self-published, 2014), https://theplanningmotive.com/Planning the Future

42. For more on this see Barry M. Richman, 'Innovation problems in Soviet industry', *Management International*, vol. 3, no. 6 (1963).

43. Leon Trotsky, *The Transitional Program for Socialist Revolution* (Pathfinder Press, 1973), p. 102.

44. Nancy Holmstrom and Richard Smith, 'The necessity of gangster capitalism: Primitive accumulation in Russia and China', *Monthly Review*, Feb. 2000.

45. 'The more easily (comparatively, of course) did the Russian proletariat pass through the revolutionary crisis, the harder

becomes now its socialist constructive work.' Leon Trotsky, 'Not by politics alone does man thrive', *Pravda*, 10 July 1923.

46. Leon Trotsky, *Where is Britain Going?* (Routledge, 1926), p. 30.

5 Debates within Socialism: Automation, UBI and Market Socialism

1. Peter Rutland, *The Myth of the Plan: Lessons of Soviet Planning Experience* (Open Court Publishing Co. 1985), p. 28.

2. John Kenneth Galbraith, *The New Industrial State* (Houghton Mifflin, 1967).

3. Adler, *The 99 percent Econ%my*.

4. Michael Rozworski and Leigh Phillips, *The People's Republic of Walmart: How the World's Biggest Corporations are Laying the Foundation for Socialism* (Verso, 2019).

5. Cottrell and Cockshott, 'Calculation, complexity and planning', p. 23.

6. David Laibman, 'Democratic coordination: Towards a working socialism for the new century', *Science & Society*, vol. 66, no. 1, special issue *Building Socialism Theoretically: Alternatives to Capitalism and the Invisible Hand* (spring 2002), p. 119.

7. For instance see Justin Joque, *Revolutionary Mathematics: Artificial Intelligence, Statistics and the Logic of Capitalism* (Verso, 2022).

8. See:http://socialistplanning.org/posts/review-peoples-republic

9. Aaron Benanav, 'How to make a pencil', *Logic(s)*, issue 12 (20 Dec. 2020).

10. Jasper Bernes, 'Planning and anarchy', *South Atlantic Quarterly*, vol. 119, no. 1 (Jan. 2020), p. 55.

11. Ibid., p. 68.

12. Eden Medina, *Cybernetic Revolutionaries: Technology and Politics in Allende's Chile* (MIT Press, 2011), p. 32.

13. Ibid., p. 34.

14. Ibid., pp. 37–8.

15. Ibid., p. 173.

16. In Greek *Alge* is sad and *Hedonic* is happy.

17. Medina, *Cybernetic Revolutionaries*, pp. 145–6.

18. Bernes, 'Planning and anarchy', p. 54.

19. Medina, *Cybernetic Revolutionaries*, pp. 174–6.

20. Ibid., p. 201.

21. Ibid., p. 180.

22. Bruce Caldwell and Leonidas Montes, 'Friedrich Hayek and his visits to Chile', *Review of Austrian Economics*, vol. 28, no. 3 (2015), pp. 261–309.

23. From the poem by Richard Brautigan:

> I like to think
> (it has to be!)
> of a cybernetic ecology
> where we are free of our labours
> and joined back to nature,
> returned to our mammal
> brothers and sisters,
> and all watched over
> by machines of loving grace.

24. V.I. Lenin, *The State and Revolution* (Progress Publishers, 1969), p. 41.

25. Smith, *Invisible Leviathan*, p. 318.

26. Mészáros, *Beyond Capital*, p. 433.

27. Guy Standing, *Basic Income: And How We Can Make It Happen* (Pelican Books, 2017).

28. Philippe Van Parijs and Yannick Vanderborght, *Basic Income: A Radical Proposal for a Free Society and a Sane Economy* (Harvard University Press, 2017).

29. Bregman, *Utopia for Realists*, pp. 25–47.

30. Brian O'Boyle, 'A socialist case against universal basic income', July 2021, www.rebelnews.ie/2021/07/05/universal-basic-income-socialist-case-against/

31. Ibid.

32. Benanav, *Automation and the Future of Work*.

33. Ibid., p. 78.

34. Bastani, *Fully Automated Luxury Socialism*, pp. 213–17.

35. UCL, 'Expanding basic services could be more effective at reducing poverty than a Universal Basic Income', May 2019, www.ucl.ac.uk/news/2019/may/expanding-basic-services-could-be-more-effective-reducing-poverty-universal-basic-income

36. 'Plan versus market', *Trotskyist Bulletin*, Oct. 1996.

37. For a very robust account of this debate see David McNally, *Against the Market: Political Economy, Market Socialism and the Marxist Critique* (Verso, 1993).

38. For more on this see Ernest Mandel's *From Stalinism to Euro-communism* (New Left Books, 1978).

39. Alec Nove, *The Economics of Feasible Socialism* (Taylor & Francis, 2013), p. 44.

40. Ibid., p. 111.

41. Ibid., p. 44.

42. For Lange, see *On the Economic Theory of Socialism*, ed. Benjamin E. Lippincott (A.M. Kelly, 1970). There isn't space to go into more of Lange and the inter-war school of market socialists but, as a brief criticism, they accepted a lot of the basis of neo-classical economics that focused on the question of distribution and prices and not on production. This led them to concede ground to the basic arguments of the anti-socialists.

43. Diane Elson, 'Market socialism or socialisation of the market?', *New Left Review*, I/172 (Nov.–Dec. 1988), p. 8.

44. Peter Rutland, *The Myth of the Plan: Lessons of Soviet Planning Experience* (Cambridge University Press, 2017), p. 3.

45. James Lawler in Bertell Ollman (ed.) *Market Socialism: The Debate Among Socialists* (Routledge, 1998). Similar arguments are in Michael Howard, *Self-management and the Crisis of Socialism* (Rowman & Littlefield, 2000). In fact similar arguments are everywhere.

46. David Schweickart, *After Capitalism* (Rowman & Littlefield, 2002).

47. Simon Hannah, *A Party with Socialists in It* (Pluto, 2022).

48. Girdin, 'Socialism for realists'.

49. McNally, *Against the Market*, p. 172.

50. Tony Andréani, 'Market socialism: Problems and models', in Jacques Bidet and Sathis Kouvlakis (eds) *Critical Companion to Contemporary Marxism* (Haymarket, 2009), pp. 239–40.

51. For more on China see Simon Hannah, *Capitalist China and Socialist Revolution* (Resistance Books, 2023).

52. Sharryn Kasmir, 'Mondragón coops and the anthropological imagination', *Focaal* blog, 29 June 2015.

53. Hudis (*Marx's Alternatives*, p. 193) makes the following point: 'workers would not have effective control of their cooperative production if an independent pricing mechanism acted in disregard of their collective deliberations by dictating the manner, form, and nature of their labouring activity'.

54. Samary, *Planning, Markets and Democracy*.

55. As Andréani argues, 'but can we speak of socialism? Are we not instead dealing with a state capitalism or a "popular" capitalism?' In 'Market socialism', p. 244.

56. Mandel, 'Economics of the transition period'.

57. Devine, *Democracy and Economic Planning*, p. 236.

58. Ibid., pp. 238–43.

59. Grunberg, 'The planning daemon'.

60. Ibid.

61. Campbell, 'Democratic planned socialism', p. 34.

6   Green New Deal, Ecosocialism and Degrowth

1. Salvage Collective, *The Tragedy of the Worker*.

2. Eric Roston et al., 'How the world's richest people are driving global warming', *Bloomberg*, 23 March 2022.

3. 'How the rich are driving climate change', *BBC News*, 28 Oct. 2021.

4. www.activesustainability.com/climate-change/100-companies-responsible-71-ghg-emissions/

5. 'Revealed: The 20 firms behind a third of all carbon emissions', *Guardian*, 9 Oct. 2019.

6. 'US military pollution: The world's biggest climate change enabler?', 12 Nov. 2021, https://earth.org/us-military-pollution/

7. Neta C. Crawford, *The Pentagon, Climate Change, and War: Charting the Rise and Fall of U.S. Military Emissions* (MIT Press, 2022), p. 117.

8. Nicholas Stern and Joseph E. Stiglitz, 'Climate change and growth: Industrial and corporate change', *Industrial and Corporate Change*, vol. 32, no. 2 (2023), p. 289.

9. Saito, *Marx in the Anthropocene*, p. 13.

10. Mandel, *Marxist Economic Theory*.

11. Löwy, *Ecosocialism*, p. 81.

12. For instance Peter A. Victor, *Managing without Growth: Slower by Design, Not Disaster* (Edward Elgar, 2008); Tim Jackson, *Prosperity without Growth: Economics for a Finite Planet* (Routledge, 2009) and Kohei Saito, *Marx in the Anthropocene*.

13. Löwy, *Ecosocialism*, pp. 83–104.

14. The concept of the Anthropocene entered mainstream discussion around 2000, pioneered by Paul J. Crutzen, an atmospheric chemist, and limnologist Eugene F. Stoermer. It has been challenged from a Marxist angle in Jason W. Moore's book *Anthropocene or Capitalocene? Nature, History, and the Crisis of Capitalism* (PM Press/Kairos, 2016) and the endorsement of it in 'Against the Anthropocene', by Daniel Hartley (in *Salvage*, 31 Aug. 2015). Saito discusses this in ch. 4 of *Marx in the Anthropocene*. The Salvage Editorial Board themselves have argued for a turn towards the Proletarocene, where working-class resistance and action is central to our survival.

15. Federico Demaria et al., 'What is degrowth? From an activist slogan to a social movement', *Environmental Values*, vol. 22, issue 2 (2013).

16. D.L. Meadows, D.H. Meadows, J. Randers and W. Behrens III, *The Limits to Growth* (Universe Books, 1972).

17. Dean Curran, 'The treadmill of production and the positional economy of consumption', *Canadian Review of Sociology*, vol. 54, no. 1 (2017), p. 30.

18. Michael Löwy, Bengi Akbulut, Sabrina Fernandes and Giorgos Kallis, 'For an ecosocialist degrowth', *Monthly Review*, 1 April 2022.

19. Dorothy Grace Guerrero, 'Degrowth and the perspectives about it from the South', Global Justice Now, 19 Sept. 2019.

20. Hickel, *Less is More*, p. 30.

21. Stern and Stiglitz, *Climate Change and Growth*, p. 286.

22. Saito, *Marx in the Anthropocene*, p. 237.

23. John Bellamy Foster et al., 'Against Doomsday scenarios: What is to be done now?', *Monthly Review*, 1 Dec. 2021.

24. Laura Cozzi et al., 'For the first time in decades, the number of people without access to electricity is set to increase in 2022', IEA 50, 3 Nov. 2022, www.iea.org/commentaries/for-

the-first-time-in-decades-the-number-of-people-without-access-to-electricity-is-set-to-increase-in-2022

25. Benanav, 'Socialist investment, dynamic planning, and the politics of human need', p. 196.

26. Saito, *Marx in the Anthropocene*, p. 237.

27. Phil Ward, 'The ecological crisis and its consequences for socialists', *Climate and Capitalism*, 14 June 2008.

28. See for instance Vettese and Pendergrass, *Half-Earth Socialism*.

29. Alexander Dunlap and Louis Laratte, 'European Green Deal necropolitics: Exploring "green" energy transition, degrowth and infrastructural colonization', *Political Geography* vol. 97 (Aug. 2022).

30. Friedrich Engels, *Dialectics of Nature*, Part IX (International Publishers, 1960), pp 291–2.

31. Nikolai Bukharin, *Historical Materialism: A System of Sociology* (University of Michigan Press, 1969), p. 104.

32. Karl Marx, 'Private property and communism', in *Economic and Philosophic Manuscripts of 1844*, *Collected Works*, vol. 3 (Lawrence & Wishart, 1975), pp. 296–7.

33. *The Guardian*, 'Few willing to change lifestyle to save the planet, climate survey finds', 7 Nov. 2021.

34. See: www.prweb.com/releases/2023/3/prweb19203037.htm, 3 March 2023. See also the section on cutting advertising in Hickel, *Less is More*.

35. Michael Löwy, 'Nine theses on ecosocialist degrowth', *Monthly Review*, July 2023.

36. Ollman, 'Marx's vision of communism: A reconstruction', p. 28.

37. Satish Raichur, 'Economic "laws", the law of value and Chinese socialism', *Australian Economic Papers*, vol. 20 (1981), p. 207.

38. Kate Soper, *Post-growth Living: For an Alternative Hedonism* (Verso, 2020), p. 179 (Ebook version).

39. Ibid.

Conclusion

1. Marx, *Economic and Philosophical Manuscripts*.

2. G.M. Gilbert, *The Psychology of Dictatorship* (The Ronald Press, 1950).

Index

Thanks to our Patreon subscriber:

Ciaran Kane

Who has shown generosity and comradeship in support of our publishing.

Check out the other perks you get by subscribing to our Patreon – visit patreon.com/plutopress.

Subscriptions start from £3 a month.

The Pluto Press Newsletter

Hello friend of Pluto!

Want to stay on top of the best radical books
we publish?

Then sign up to be the first to hear about our
new books, as well as special events,
podcasts and videos.

You'll also get 50% off your first order with us
when you sign up.

Come and join us!

Go to bit.ly/PlutoNewsletter